In loving memory of Manorama...

Foreward 1

*GOOD GOVERNACE AND LEADERSHIP PERSPECTIVES
-     OF CORPORATIONS… AND OF THE UNIVERSE!*

I have had the opportunity of knowing the authors over many years.

Sushil worked in the manufacturing and maintenance industry for over 3 decades, has experienced corporate management up close and personal.

He has traveled extensively across various parts of the world, and experienced people and religious beliefs and practices.

He has also authored a number of books across a variety of topics such as Maintenance Engineering, Career, Counseling, Healing and Meditation.

Sushil has good command in describing science, spirituality and environment. He defines divinity as the basis for good governance.

This book explores parallels between Governance of Corporations and the Governance of the Universe.

We have all wondered how the world came to be. And how it runs. How circle of life continues. Good deeds are recognized over time, and poor deeds punished. By God, by governments, by company management. Successful companies and not so successful companies. Good corporate management and those that could do better.

I found this book to be very interesting. It draws a compelling bridge between religious practices, constraints and beliefs and corporate practices, constraints and beliefs. It is meticulous in its research and grounded in decades of deep thinking and observation of how the world runs.

I recommend this book for those who are interested to learn about hinduism. About religion. About corporations. About governance. About why our ancestors told us to certain things certain way. About the fallacy of 330 million gods. About the laws of karma and the Newton's laws of motion. And the notion of "Maya" and the blockbuster series "Matrix Trilogy".

The authors have explored various concepts of Hindu mythology, Hinduism, India, Bharat and Bhartiya. Explored its evolution over the time and implicit relationships in broad sense. A lifetime is not enough to study all documented hindu scriptures as there are 4 Vedas, 18 Puranas, 108 Upnishads, 6 shashtras, Manu samriti, Yoga Sutra, Ramayana and Mahabharatha (Mahabhartha is considered 5th Veda). But this is a serious work, with ample research to explain practices and to draw parallels to the corporate world, to learn from, and to improve operations.

The book starts out with a rich glimpse of Hinduism. It contrasts the Universe versus Corporations, and dwells upon governance concepts. Then it takes on the complex concepts of Creation, Running & Preservation, and dissolution of Corporations and of Life in the universe.

This is a valuable book and is a key for many queries regarding governance of the universe. I congratulate the author for such a wonderful gift The Corporate Governance of the Universe.

Prof. Nilu Gupta
De Anza College
Cupertino, CA
2020

Foreward 2

Dear readers of "The Corporate Governance of the Universe",

Growing up in the Silicon Valley at the heart of technological innovation, I've always had a urge to question the functionality of any system I didn't fully understand. When my grandfather, the author of this novel, asked me to write a foreword, I jumped at the opportunity. The concept intrigued me - a thorough analysis of the inner workings and functionality of the universe through the lens of Hinduism, and in contrast with the governance of corporations. I am delighted to have the opportunity to foreword this novel.

Being a 17 year old member of Generation Z, I began reading this novel with the perspective of a teenager born and raised in America. I've never studied Hinduism or engaged in it more deeply than having a mild interest in it. As such, before reading this novel, I was relatively unable to associate with the theme of Hindu mythology and its applications and linkages to our daily lives. I didn't expect to be able to connect with the message of the novel and the deities described in it. The further I got into the novel, however, the more I began to connect with its contents. I realized that there were distinct connections between this novel and mainstream American media material.

*One such example of this is the **Avengers**. The diversely powerful individuals on the Avenger team all possess different supernatural abilities and operate with the collective goal of protecting the Earth. To the Hindu reader, the Avengers can almost seem to be direct manifestations of the Hindu deity system, considering they also consists of a plethora of gods, all with the goal to oversee life in the universe. The underlying parallels between Indian mythology and the superhero media may have been what resulted in "Avengers Endgame" becoming the highest grossing film of 2019 in India.*

Although I began reading this novel with a limited appreciation of Hindu deities and religion, as I finished it, my eyes opened and I began to see connections to spirituality in my daily life. As you read this novel, try to think about the connections and implications that you see that may be applicable to your daily lives. I assure you that even those feeling rather distant from Hindu mythology, as I initially did, can find themselves in this novel, tying their own cultural beliefs and ideals to those of Hinduism. This novel, and the broad spectrum of topics it attempts to cover, is relevant to everyone -from well-read religious experts to mildly curious individuals with little to no past involvement with religion.

I encourage you to continue on, and read this novel with an open mind. Try your best to ask questions and draw connections. This book is most powerful when the reader uses it to embrace their spirituality and connect and question the inner-workings of our universe. I hope this book will change your perspective on Hinduism and the Universe and its workings like it did for me.

Arjun Gupta
Co-founder and Executive president at Elevate the Future
Co-founder and CFO at HorusML
San Jose, CA
2020

Preface

At outset, the authors confess that they are neither space scientist / scholar nor they are serious religious / spiritual preachers, yet they have ventured to write this book, simply on the strength of one famous quote, i.e. *'Every Indian is a born philosopher'*.

The question 'where from and how did we, the living being, came to this planet, 'Earth' has been haunting the minds of both general people and scientists, since ages. Did we evolve from simple inorganic matters, as per Darwin's theory and if that is possible or scientifically proven? Or did we come as alien from another planet, which was already inhabited by beings? Or were we created by some unimaginable all powerful and all resourceful supreme power, known as God, Brahman, Maha-Vishnu, Allah and so on, which again is hypothetical?

Again, we know that for running any big corporation or corporate entity efficiently, sound management and governing principles and practices are needed. Our universe, such an enormous entity / organization, has been running in somewhat similar pattern since ages. Seasons come and go, sun rises in east and sets in west, people get born, live and die and even the so-called natural calamities, like cyclones and tsunamis also occur somewhat patterned. Innumerable planets and galaxies do not fall apart but move in somewhat patterned manner. Are all these possible without the guidance / governance of any supreme power(s)?

The book tries to answer or deal with few of such questions. The main purpose of writing this book is to explore with the readers (everyone in our society— one and all) and for readers that how such a gigantic and diverse universe is being governed almost meticulously and how it can be compared with the governance of an enormous organization, corporation or corporate entity. The book attempts to show the reasonable parallelism in governance of universe by Gods and deities and that of any big corporation by human. At no place the book discusses the religious practices, ethics, behaviors, sermons, veneration and festivals etc. As such, the book shouldn't be considered as a religious book, but as a book for general reading.

The book mentions the gods / goddesses / deities mainly from Hinduism, simply because authors knowledge is limited to Hinduism. However, at many places broad comparison has been given with other religions, mythologies and cultures. Of-course, the readers knowledgeable about other religions/mythologies, can extrapolate this book with gods / deities of their own religion / mythologies.

The organization of the book is in six self-contained chapters. It starts with a brief glimpse of Hinduism--- how the words Hindu and Hinduism originated, essence of its philosophy, showing its vastness as well as simplicity and telling that Hinduism is not only a religion but is a way of life and state of mind and how it complements science, its gods and deities and the Timeline for Hinduism. This chapter also gives a hint of influence of Hinduism on Hollywood movies.

Chapter-2 discusses universe vis-à-vis corporation— what is universe, from both, scientific and mythological lenses, what is corporation and corporate governance / management, comparison between universe and corporation with respect to their constituents, ingredients and challenges. It also gives a brief overview of cycle of universe, multi-universe or omniverse, Big-Bang, Big-Crunch and Big-Bounce.

Chapter-3 gives a brief overview of the title of the book, i.e. Corporate Governance of the Universe. It shows the similarities between the corporate style governance of universe and corporate style governance / management of any corporation or corporate entity. It extends such similarity of governance of universe with governance of a country, governance of word 'Aum / Om' and even governance of 'life-cycle of human being'.

Chapter-4 explores similarities of creation aspects of universe and corporation, i.e. 'who', 'why' and 'how' aspects of creation of universe, from both, scientific and mythological lenses and how do these compare with that of any corporation or corporate entity. It gives Timeline for Evolution of Universe and Mankind, Formation / Evolution of Universe, Emergence / Evolution of Life on Earth and Evolution of Universe thru Prakriti. It also discusses Darwinian theory vis-à-vis Hinduism Philosophy and Hindu Mythology vis-à-vis other mythologies about creation aspects.

Chapter-5 discusses current Universe Time Division and Lord Vishnu's Model of preservation of a corporate entity as well as universe, taking use of Life-Cycle Management (LCM) and Terotechnology. It also shows Lord Vishnu's way of preservation of universe thru various avatars, for all three types of care, i.e. general care, advanced care and intensive care, in line with Terotechonology. It also gives the organization chart of Lord Vishnu.

Chapter-6, starts with Panchanana (5- Aspects) of Shiva as per Shaivism and why Lord Shiva is, mostly, worshipped as Lingam. It, then, discusses the "Why" and "How" aspects of Lord Shiva's responsibility as in-charge of destruction and dissolution and, also, Shiva's way of working vis-a-vis Corporate I/c General Administration. It shows Shiva's management of contradicting attributes and its usefulness in management of any corporate entity. Shiva's family is unique and gives a great message. Shiva's organization chart further explains these. It explains the difference between Vishnu as destroyer of evil-doers Shiva as destroyer of evildoers. Lastly, it gives broad comparison of three faces / forms of Brahman and their impact in our daily life.

Regarding readership, the book is useful and worth reading by everyone— one and all, i.e. people from all walks of life.

Reasonable help of sketches / figures and tables have been taken to explain the topics. Some places may appear somewhat repetitious, but this has been done intentionally to further emphasize certain points.

A unique feature of this book is down to earth practicality and simplicity of complex topics. The authors have presented the concepts with simple usable techniques and methods which the readers can easily understand and apply in their workaday world.

The authors express their sincere thanks and gratitude to all authors and publishers mentioned in bibliography / references which have worked as source of knowledge. The authors also express thanks and gratitude to all other persons who, directly or indirectly, helped or advised in preparation of this book.

Just around the end of preparation of manuscript, the co-author, Mrs. Manorama Srivastava (who happened to be my wife also) left this world for her Heavenly abode. As such, all further communication will be done by me, the first author.

SUSHIL KUMAR SRIVASTAVA

Table of Contents

1   Introduction & Glimpse of Hinduism

(Hindus and Hindutva will one day rule the world, because this is a combination of knowledge and wisdom --- Leo Tolstoy)

At the outset, the authors again confess that they are neither space scientists / scholars nor they are serious religious / spiritual preachers, yet they have ventured to write this book, simply on the strength of one famous quote, i.e. *'Every Indian is a born philosopher'*. The authors also agree that they may not be adequately qualified to talk or write anything about our Gods or the space science and universe. What the authors have done in this book is to draw a parallel and outward similarity in management and governance of big corporations/industries and supposedly governance of our universe by our Gods. As such, this book may not be considered as a religious book.

As the author (Sushil) is basically of engineering background, the book attempts to give an analytical and graphical depiction of the narrations and author (Manorama) has been a teacher and a sociologist, the book also gives a social and cultural perspective, with a simplistic touch.

While drawing the parallels between the governance of universe and governance of a business / industrial corporates, the book mentions Gods, Goddesses and deities of Hindu mythology only. This does not belittle other faiths, cultures and mythologies but only indicates that the authors' knowledge is limited to Hindu mythology and, as such, authors have not ventured to mention the Gods and deities of other faiths, cultures and mythologies. Of-course, at some places, comparison of Hindu mythology with other mythologies have been given.

As almost all the Gods / deities, referred to in this book have been taken from Hinduism, we would first discuss briefly about Hindu & Hinduism.

Knowledge for discussion can be derived either thru 'Descending Channel' or 'Ascending Channel'. In 'Descending Channel' (e.g. Vedic Channel) knowledge comes from previous authorities and assuming that, further development may be done. In 'Ascending Channel' (also known as Scientific Channel, approach / process) of knowledge, scientists, generally, don't accept prior authorities, except of other similar scientists and try to uncover the mysteries thru their own perceptions / assumptions / derivations, backed by various instruments, equipment and, also, using mathematical approaches to verify their theories / derivations. However, if one pursues meticulously to its ultimate conclusion, its result will not be much different from those achieved by descending approach. In this book, we would be considering both channels, with little more emphasis on descending channel.

1.1   Origin of words 'Hindu' and 'Hinduism'

The word Hindu does not appear anywhere in the Hindu scriptures, viz, Vedas, Upanishads, and Puranas, not even in 'Ramayana' and 'Mahabharat'. According to Sir Monier Williams, the Sanskrit lexicographer, you cannot find an indigenous root for the words Hindu or India. In those literatures, people have been identified as Sanatanis (Sanatan Dharma) or Aryans. Another word, which described more accurately about the people of present Indian Sub-continent, is Bhaaratiya. People of India are believed to be the descendants of King Bharat. From his name comes the original name of India, Bhaarat, and, those residing in Bhaarat are Bhaaratiya.

The word 'Hindu' appears to come from the Sanskrit word Sindhu which is the original name for the Indus River that flows through the north-western part of the Indian subcontinent. Most of the people, from other part of the world, came through this route in search of the then famous 'land of golden bird' and encountered the so called 'Indus civilization'. One of the earliest travelers, the Greeks, used the word 'Indu', based on River Indus (Sindhu), and later simplified as "Hindu', to denote the country and people living beyond the Indus river. Megasthenes' historical book 'Indica' epitomizes the name for India and Indians around the 4th Century B.C.E. Persian King Darious-1 (who extended his empire up to the borders of the Indian subcontinent in 517 BC) and Alexander the Great, around 325 BC, both contributed to renaming the River Sindhu as the Indu, dropping the beginning "S", thus making it easier for the Persians / Greeks to pronounce and thus paved the way for calling people east of River Sindhu as "Indian".

This word 'Indu' was misunderstood by Arabs, Muslim invaders, and few medieval Historians, as they could not pronounce the word "Indu" and, as such, simplified as "Hindu'. However, this was only an extension of the name used by the Greeks. The Arabic term 'al-Hind', referred to the land of the people who live across the river Indus. By the 13th century, the world Hindustan began to be used as a popular alternative name for India, meaning the "land of Hindus". Around 18th century, the European merchants and colonists referred collectively to the followers of the Dharmic religions (presently known as Hinduism, Buddhism, Sikhism and Jainism) in Hindustan — which geographically referred to most parts of the northern Indian subcontinent — as Hindus. Eventually, any person of Indian origin who did not practice Abrahamic religions (Judaism, Christianity and Islam) came to be known as a Hindu, thereby encompassing a wide range of religious beliefs and practices. Nehru, in his book, 'Discovery of India' also states that the earliest reference to the term Hindu was found in the Tantrik (Hinduism /Buddhism) literatures of the 8th century AD.

With the word 'Hindu', the word 'ism' was added (to make the word Hinduism), in nineteenth century by Britishers and English writers to denote the culture and religion of the high-caste Brahmans and people of other casts. The word Hinduism was soon adopted by the Hindus themselves, as a term that encompassed their national, social and cultural identity. It is also said that Hinduism developed from the religion that the Aryans brought to India with them in about 1500 BC. Its beliefs and practices are based on the Vedas, a collection of hymns (thought to refer to actual historical events) that Aryan scholars had completed by about 800 BC. Today, Hinduism encompasses, along with other things, all the Vedic and ancient literatures / scriptures.

1.2   What is Hinduism

The subject is very vast, but we would discuss here in very brief. A famous judgment pronounced in December 1995 by a three Judge Bench of the Supreme Court of India (headed by Justice Thakur), in connection of use of "Hindutva" as a slogan during an election campaign, had pronounced that "Hindutva is not a religion, but a way of life and a state of mind". Later, few other leaders also corroborated that 'Hinduism is not a religion, but a way of life and state of mind'. This concept arises because Hinduism is least restrictive, least authoritative, least punitive, least demanding and extremely liberal and accommodating. You may or may not worship a deity or perform any 'puja' or listen to any spiritual leader--- nobody will question you or sermon you. Some Hindus are only 'spiritual' (believes in existence of God), but not necessarily 'religious' (participate in religious activities). Hindus always accommodated few new branches of worship and religion and are given permission to accept and reject any method or every method of worship, or even reject God.

Another way to argue that the Hinduism is not a religion in line with other religions is that most other religions were started by some prophet (Christianity by Jesus Christ, Islam by Prophet Mohammad, Buddhism by Gautam Buddha, Confucianism by Confucius and so on), but there was no such prophet to start Hinduism (Sanatan Dharma or Vedic religion). There is no central authority in Hinduism, and no one can pass an order to excommunicate you. Again, in most other religions (Abrahamic / Semitic etc.), people are, generally, God fearing, but in Hinduism, people are God loving (bhakti) and no fear psychosis. Fear psychosis is, generally, negative, but love and bhakti are positive. Famous American teacher and author, Dr. David Frawley has said, "The beauty of Hindu Dharma is that it is not a man-made historical religion, dependent upon a church, a savior or prophet, or preaching any belief or dogma; Hindu Dharma rises from Earth, from our inner Being and allows us to embrace the entire universe with us."

However, in true sense, Hinduism has become a religion, taking its philosophies and rituals etc. from Vedas, Upanishads, Puranas and other scriptures and teachings from various rishis and gurus. Swamy Vivekananda had publicly announced that "Hinduism is the mother of all religions" and, also, Lokmanya Tilak clearly stated in 'Gita Rahasya' that Hinduism is a religion. As pointed out by Changrath Vikram on the Internet, Hinduism has all the necessary attributes to classify it as a religion, namely common scriptures like Vedas, the Gita, the Ramayana and several other holy texts, a common mode of worship, common temples and a number of deities uniformly worshipped by all Hindus.

The vastness of Hinduism can be visualized from an instance that while Hinduism is trying to capture a total 360 degrees view of an elephant, other religions are, probably, happy capturing only a part of the elephant, staying with that and, thus, limiting their views. Authors' this view is, again, without any intention to belittle other religions. Because of its vastness, Hinduism is also a very pragmatic religion and myths are often used to address a phenomenon and not the other way around.

Hinduism is a conglomeration of distinct intellectual or philosophical points of view, rather than a rigid common set of beliefs. The essence of Hinduism is "all inclusive", i.e. it's ability to assimilate every good thing from everything / anywhere. It has taken cue from Rig Veda's saying, --"Ano bhadrah Krathavo Yanthu Vishwathah", i.e. let the knowledge come to us from every direction. That is why it is eternal. It has withstood the test of time in-spite of repeated onslaught both from within and outside. Hinduism is a fusion of philosophy and religion, a deep wisdom and a concern with the ultimate, that had no parallel in either contemporary Western philosophy or Western religion.

There are four goals for a typical / average person in Hinduism (not for a saint or priest) ---Dharma, Artha, Kama, and Moksha. Dharma is right action. This is the moral code and ethics, fulfilling the duties of one's position. Artha is the gathering of wealth. Wealth should be gathered for helping others and to remove barriers to dharmic living. Kama is the joy of sexual desire and is to be celebrated (normally within marriage). As energy is never created or destroyed, Hindus believe that the human soul travels through different lifetimes, until it is ready to merge with the Infinite God from which it came. Liberation from the cycle of death and rebirth is Moksha and is the ultimate goal of Hindu life. More about this later in next sections.

1.3   Glimpse God and Atman

We may term God by names like 'Brahman' 'Almighty', 'Supreme Power' 'Ultimate Reality', 'ॐ', 'Trinity', 'Shiva', 'Allah' and so on, but that supreme God is only one and the same. Different religions are merely different roads / paths to the God; though we can achieve the same without any religion. Few revered saints / sages of most religions / faiths had a vision of God as self-luminous light with an oval aura or in any other shape or image as per their beliefs. Swamy Vivekananda had said, "God is a circle whose circumference is nowhere and whose center is everywhere; man is also an infinite circle whose circumference is nowhere, but whose center is located in a spot." As per Hinduism, God is omniscient (all-knowing), omnipotent (all-powerful), omnipresent (present everywhere), omnibenevolent (all-loving), 'nirakar' (formless), 'nirvikar' (imperturbable), 'nirgun' (without distinction/ qualities), 'niranjan' (spotless/pure), 'ananta' (infinite) and 'sacchidananda' (supreme consciousness & bliss), as shown in Fig. 1.1. As such, it is difficult to define God. We often say that God is 'neti-neti' (not this not that). He is greater than the greatest, smaller than the smallest and is also inmost 'Self' of all. He sees, hears and knows everything, although none can see, hear and know him. He sees all beings in Himself and Himself in all beings. God is the indwelling 'Spirit' in man and nature. The whole universe is filled with the spirit of God. He is the Lord of universe--- the universe rises out of him, is supported by him and gets dissolved back into him. He is also known as "pure consciousness" and contains in itself both, being and non-being.

As per Vedas, God is the entire universe itself, and this universe extends into the infinity well beyond the physical universe which we see, feel and live in--- in the form of stars, planets, galaxies and inter-galactic stuff, all of which that was created during the so called 'big bang'. God existed even before the so called 'big bang'. The physical universe, which we live in, is a temporary phenomenon created in 'big bang' and which has an end and exists within the real universe which is nothing but God. So, in other words, we all live inside the God, and we are a part of the God itself (Aham Brahmasmi, i.e. I am God). We should put God in everything and conduct our life, enjoy our life, in and through God.

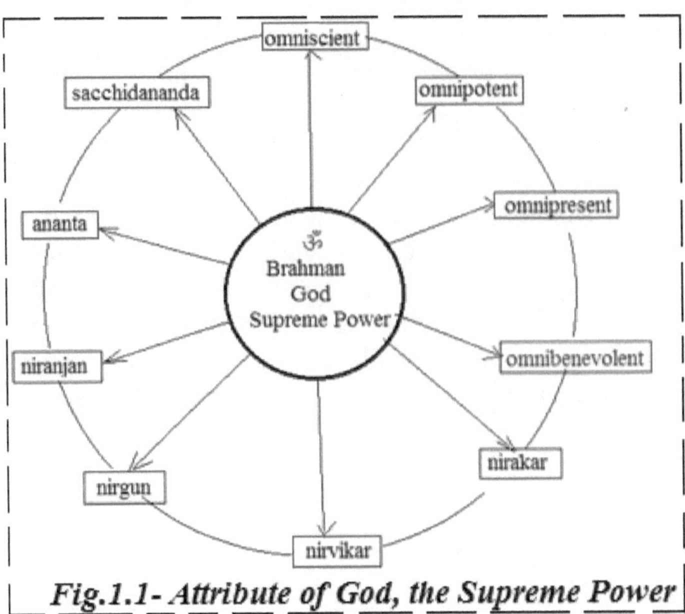

Fig.1.1- Attribute of God, the Supreme Power

1.3.1   Masculine Energy- Feminine Energy Concept

As it is little confusing for average person to visualize the
'nirakar', 'nirgun', 'anant' God, Upanishads, sometimes, describe
him as "Purusha" (the divine being in Human form), to help us
meditate upon him, more easily. As commoners understand that
a combination of male and female makes creation, scriptures
mentioned a consort of 'Purusha' as 'Prakriti'. Purusha literally
means "man" and Prakriti literally means "creatrix," the female
creative energy. Purusha did not create Prakriti but is responsible
for Prakriti becoming animated, alive. Purusha is pure
consciousness and ever existing, but Prakriti is that which is
created, and it is nature in all her aspects. As such, Brahman, the
supreme power is an amalgamation of these two forms. Some
scriptures mention 'Shiva' and 'Shakti' as Purusha and Prakriti.
We know that Purusha, the Shiva, is constant, but Prakriti has
taken different names /forms as Parvati, Sati or Shakti etc.

Since every individual is a part of the God itself (Aham
Brahmasmi), Purusha and Prakriti or Shiva and Shakti can also
be visualized as 'masculine energy' and 'feminine energy',
appearing separate, but inseparable. In other words, God can be
considered in two portions, masculine (Purusha) and feminine
(Prakriti)---- something similar to the 'Ardhanarishwara'- a
composite androgynous form of the Hindu God Shiva and his
consort Parvati. Creation is possible only when they are together
as one inseparable reality. Ardhanarishvara is a popular
iconographic form found in many Shiva temples throughout
India and it represents the synthesis of masculine and feminine
energies of the universe (Purusha and Prakriti) and illustrates
how Shakti, the female principle of God, is inseparable from
Shiva, the male principle of God. Fig. 1.2 shows this aspect.

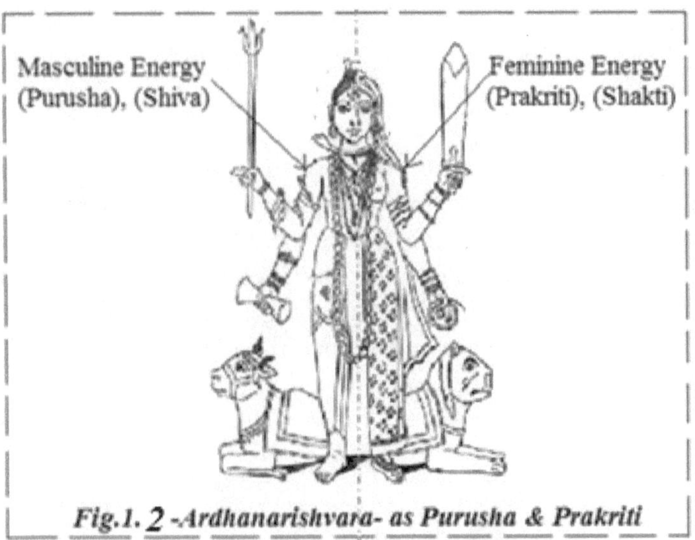

Fig.1. 2 -Ardhanarishvara- as Purusha & Prakriti

The masculine energy (Purusha) is somewhat aggressive / active and hot and corresponds to sun, light and fire etc. and the feminine energy (Prakriti) is somewhat passive and cold and corresponds to moon, darkness, earth and water etc. In the Bhagawad Gita, Lord Krishna describes these concepts as 'Kshetra' and 'Kshetragna'. The term 'Kshetra' means 'arena or field of activity' and corresponds to 'Prakriti' and the 'Obvious Universe' at the global level and to the human body at the individual level. The term 'Kshetragna' refers to the 'Motivating Force or the Knower of that Field' and refers to Purusha or Brahman.

Fig. 1.3 shows this aspect in two more concepts- Chinese Yin-Yang concept and Indian Yoni-Linga concept. In Chinese philosophy, Yin-Yang is, sometime, considered as "dark-bright", "negative-positive" also, but we would consider only the "Feminine- Masculine" meaning. The 'yoni' upon which the 'lingam' often sits represents the manifest universal energy. The 'yoni', which is a symbol of Shakti, combines with the 'lingam' and becomes a symbol of the eternal union of the paternal and maternal principles, or the positive and negative, or the static and dynamic energies of the Absolute Reality. It is the communion of the eternal consciousness and dynamic power of the Shakti, the source of all actions and changes. Both, the 'Yin-Yang' and 'Yoni-Linga' concepts mean the two halves that together complete wholeness.

Again, considering God in individuals, the duality of Yoni-Linga or Yin-Yang or 'feminine-masculine' energies can also be considered as 'Ida' nadi and 'Pingla' nadi (channels / meridians), spiraling their way around spine, in the energy body of human. Ida refers to the yin energies while pingala refers to the yang energies. Bringing a balance between the Ida and Pingala will make us effective in the world.

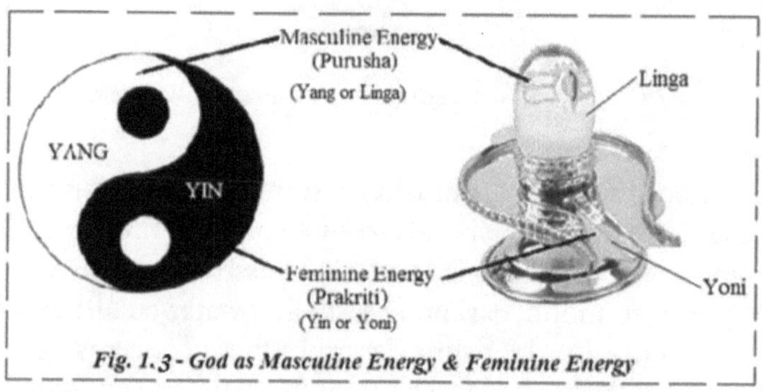

Fig. 1.3 - God as Masculine Energy & Feminine Energy

1.3.2   Atman- Jivatma

Again, as God is both, 'Him' and 'Self' (Atman), let us discuss briefly 'Atman'. Atman (the soul, the self) is the abiding spirit (the spiritual life principle of the universe), behind the body and mind of every living being. It is pure consciousness, immutably homogeneous and infinite and is the only 'Reality'. Atman is unborn and eternal. It is neither born, nor does it die with the birth and death of physical body. Atman is a part of Brahman and gets assimilated in him after death of body. It is different from the body, the senses, the prana (life force), the mind and the ego sense etc. It clearly perceives that all the bonds of his heart, which had him tied down to the mundane existence, had been broken down. All of these are enlivened by 'Him', made to work by 'Him', and for 'Him'.

However, it is also true that Atman has been encased and bound within this corporal body frame and has lost some of its freedom. In this state, it is called "Jivatma" or sometime "Jiva" in short. The reason why "Jivatma" has come to this state is individual's "Karma", the inexorable consequences of his past actions. His involvement in cycle of birth, death and rebirth, associated with consequent sufferings, is called "Samsara". The belief in samsara is closely connected to the theory of Karma which states that every action has a consequence. The previous life experience determines the present which in turn determines the future course of action. The soul (jiva) passes through different paths, experience the consequences of their activities and re-takes place (reborn) as different persons / creatures depending on the code of conduct in previous life. Bhagavad Gita also tells that "As the embodied soul continually passes, in this body, from boyhood to youth to old age, the soul similarly passes into another body at death". The endless life cycle can be terminated by moksha (salvation) – the liberation from this cycle by uniting with God. Moksha or liberation from this bondage can be achieved by 'gyana' (knowledge) and 'bhakti' (devotion), including upasana (meditation). Of-course, good Karma (Nishkam Karma, also called as 'Akarma', i.e. actions with complete detachment to the fruits of actions), as mentioned in Gita and other scriptures, is an aid for ultimate goal. After achieving Moksha, the 'Jivatma' becomes "Jivanmukta" (liberated, while still living in body). As per one view (Advaita), the 'Jivatma", after being liberated, merges into supreme Atman, also known as "Paramatma" (Brahmana, the Supreme Self, the indwelling spirit) and the physical body and subtle body disintegrates into death and gets absorbed into five basic elements. As per another view (Dvaita), the liberated 'Jivatma', (soul) travels to abode of Brahmana (Brahamlok, also known as Satyalok) and resides there permanently in infinite peace and bliss and never return to mundane existence.

For 'Jivatma' of other persons of the world, who are not liberated, Upanishads makes two categories— first category consists of those, who do 'sakam karma' (desire motivated actions, apparently appearing selfish, but with the expectation and motivation that goodness will return to him in this life) and practice some amount of 'upasana', go to 'swarg lok' (heaven), from where they would return back to this world after exhausting the results of their good deeds (karmas). The second category consists of those who did 'Vikarma' (bad and forbidden karmas / deeds) and they return and reborn again and again, as human, animals or even worms, according to the extent of their 'vikarmas'.

1.4   Hinduism Philosophy

Philosophy of Hinduism is very vast and part of which have already been discussed in previous paras. Theoretically, Hinduism philosophy refers to a group of 'darsanas' (philosophies, teachings) that emerged in ancient India. These include six systems (ṣaḍdarśana) — Sankhya, Yoga, Nyaya, Vaisheshika, Mimamsa and Vedanta. As per Vedanta school of Hindu philosophy, the concept of 'Self' (Soul) and Brahman can be considered in three ways—Advaita (monism or non-dualism, propagated by Adi Shankaracharya), Dvaita (Dualism-propagated by Madhvacharya) and Vishishtadvaita (qualified monism, propagated by Ramanuja). 'Advaita' says that both the individual self (Jivatma) and Brahman are the same and Brahman is the ultimate reality and the world is illusory (Maya). Ignorance of the reality causes suffering, and liberation can be obtained only by true knowledge of Brahman. Dvaita says that Brahman and Atman (Jivatma) are two different entities (i.e. Jivatma are many and Paramatma/ Brahman is one) and Bhakti as the route to eternal liberation. Even after liberation, the soul does not merge in Brahman, but rests in separate heavenly abode (Satya Lok) and doesn't come back to 'mrityulok'. Refer Sec.1.3.2. Vishishtadvaita says that while Brahman is the unified whole, he is characterized by multiple forms. God is the whole universe and matter and souls form his body. As such, God is viewed as the cause and, also, as the effect. It is a qualified monism, where God alone exists, but it admits plurality of souls. It is midway between Advaita and Dvaita.

However, simply stated, the Hinduism philosophy is depicted in a sort of flow diagram in Fig.1.4. The figure is self-explanatory and considers the common but important aspects of Hinduism and shows its flexibility and tolerance. As example, remaining Hindu, you may believe in God (Astik) or not (Nastik). Again, while remaining Astik, if you worship idols, you are 'Saakar Brahman' (God in some shape) worshiper otherwise you are a 'Niraakaar Brahman' (formless God) worshiper; if you take part in religious activities, you are 'religious' otherwise you are still 'spiritual'; if you like, you can read religious scriptures, if not, you can follow Bhakti (devotion) to God and if you don't want to do that also, you can simply do your Karma and so on. Hinduism believes in Vasudhaiva Kutumbakam (the world is one family) and Sarve Bhavantu Sukhinah (may all live happy). Otherwise, the Fig.1.4 is self-explanatory.

It can be said that anyone in any position can be a Hindu and can practice and benefit from its teachings. It does not matter whether one is Indian, or a Westerner born outside India, one can still adopt the Vedic / Hinduism teachings or incorporate them into his or her life for many benefits. There are no limitations in its teachings regarding who can join in. All that is required is sincerity. Hinduism accepts that everyone has the right to choose one's own path of enlightenment or salvation. In nutshell, Hinduism opens the door to the real meaning of life.

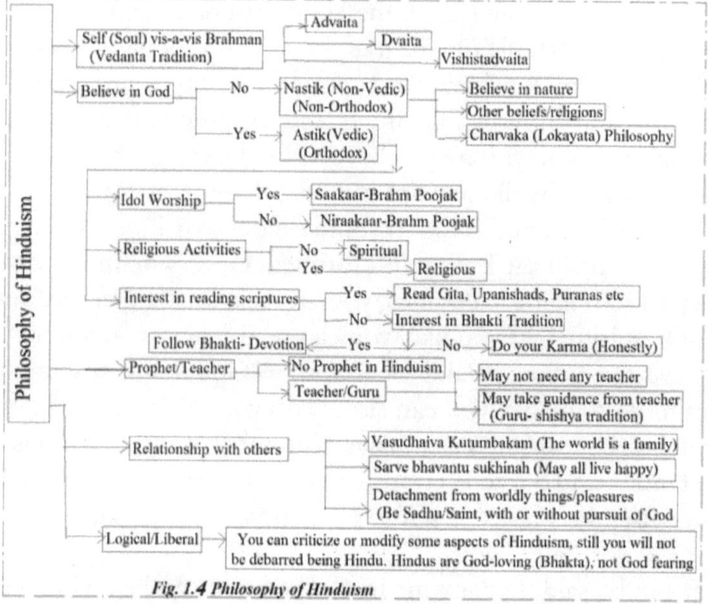

Fig. 1.4 Philosophy of Hinduism

1.4.1 Few Basic Facts about Hinduism

Few of the other basic facts about Hinduism are given below---

1- Hinduism is the world's oldest known religion, with roots going back 10,000 years and Hindu Literature (starting Rig Veda) dating back to 1200 BCE. The Vedas and many other teachings of Hinduism were preserved for thousands of years without paper. They were chanted, memorized and passed on to the next generations.

2- Around 1 billion people follow Hinduism, which is 3rd most populous religion of world, with 16% of followers. About 85% of them live in India.

3- The final goal of life in Hinduism is to attain salvation, or moksha, i.e. freedom from cycle of birth and death. Hindus believe the purpose of life is to attain self-realization or enlightenment.

4- Dharma (righteousness), Artha (means of money), Kama
(right desire), and Moksha (salvation), make up the 4
main lifegoals of Hinduism. It doesn't consider pursuit
of wealth (thru right means) a sin.

5- Hinduism, mostly, believe in only one God, but in many
forms. Hinduism is not truly polytheism. There are three
major sects in Hinduism--- Shaiva, Shakti, and
Vaishnava, but there is no strictness in following one or
other. Some advocate a fourth sect as 'Smarta', which
sees all the deities as an equal reflection of the one God,
rather than as distinct beings. They usually worship five
gods, Vishnu, Shiva, Ganesh, Surya and Devi (Shakti),
but treat them equally. Again, both, male and female
deities are worshipped with equal reverence in Hinduism.

6- Theists and Atheists are known to coexist peacefully
since time immemorial in Hinduism.

7- Om (Aum) is believed to be the manifestation of
consciousness in sound form.

8- Hinduism believe in circular, rather than linear, concept
of time. Time is divided into four ages - the Satya Yuga
(golden age of innocence), Tretha Yuga, Dwapara Yuga
and Kali Yuga and repetition continues. At the end of
Kali-Yuga, all human will die in an apocalypse (great
deluge) and, then, humanity will start with new Satya
Yuga.

9- Hinduism believe in reincarnation, i.e. the soul is
immortal, but takes on the form of many bodies until
they achieve enlightenment.

10- Mahabharata, one of the most revered books of India, is
10 times larger than the Iliad and Odyssey, combined
together.

11- Buddhism, Sikhism and Jainism are sort of derivatives
from Hinduism.

12- In Hinduism, 108 is a sacred and auspicious number.
This number also connects the Sun, Moon, and Earth.
The average distance of the Sun and the Moon from
Earth is 108 times their respective diameters.

13- Decimals, Zero, Infinity, Pi, Yoga, Pranayama,
Meditation, Vastu, Jyotish, Tantra, Astrology etc.
originated in it, with huge contributions to the world.

14- The full Kumbha-mela, a spiritual gathering of all,
occurring every 12th year at Allahabad in India, is the
largest gathering of human beings in the world. In
January 2013, over 12 crore people took bath (over 3
crores on single day on February 10, 2013) in river
Ganga. UNESCO has given Kumbha-mela an intangible
cultural heritage of humanity.

1.4.2   Vedanta compliments science

Vedanta literally means end of Vedas, which contain
philosophical essence / goal of all four Vedas. Vedanta
comprises three main scriptures—Upanishads, Bramha Sutras
and Bhagwat Gita. Its moral teachings are also explained thru
analogies in great Indian epics - Ramayana and Mahabharata.
They are the foundation of the Indian philosophy of life.

Vedanta is also known as the Science of Spirituality. It goes
beyond the laws of physical world and depicts few universal
philosophies for leading a sustainable life such as belief in action
and consequences (Law of Karma) rather than right or wrong
actions. It is not a belief system, an ideology, dogma, or a
religion; it is a method for exploring the nature of reality.
Vedantic approach (science) and modern science (mainly started
by Westerners) are neither contradictory nor incompatible. The
difference lies mainly in their vocabulary, interpretation,
methods of approach, and levels of development. Both, Vedanta

and modern science, follow the similar steps when exploring the observable universe, i.e. observe some aspect or behavior of the universe, collect information and make an educated prediction of what is taking place, known as a hypothesis, test the hypothesis with an experiment, find the results of the experiment and draw conclusion. While science has its own ways of experimenting, Vedanta's ways of experimenting is four folds—

- Bhakti Yoga – the path of feeling,
- Gyana Yoga – the path of thinking,
- Karma Yoga – the path of action,
- Raja Yoga – the path of being; the yoga of meditation and all its integrated disciplines.

Given below are few of the similarities between modern science and Vedantic approach—

1- Law of Karma vis-a-vis Newton's Law- Law of Karma states that the world is a cycle of cause and effect. One has to face the consequences of one's action in one form or the other, in one life or next life. It is somewhat similar to Newton's third law (every action has an equal and opposite reaction) and law of conservation of energy (energy can neither be created or destroyed; it can only be transformed from one form to another).

2- Energy Field- Vedanta says that material world is "Maya' (a single form of energy field created from perception- called as "prana"). Science says that material world is three fundamental energies- a combination of electric and magnetic energies, gravitational energy and nuclear energies and science is still working on a 'united field (energy) theory' combining all the three.

3- Cosmology- As per modern science, the universe, before 'Big Bang' was in point-like state with infinite temperature. With a sudden big bang, the energy was thrown out which subsequently led to the formation of stars and galaxies. Vedanta (Bhagwat Gita) also describes a cyclic universe as "All embodied beings emanate from the Unmanifest at the commencement of Brahma's day; at the commencement of his night (after around 4.3 billion years), they merge in the same subtle body of Brahma, known as the Unmanifest". This is somewhat similar to "Big Bang" and "Big Crunch" of the universe, as per modern science.

4- Medical Diagnosis- Modern science determines the abnormality of health of a person by finding the abnormality in blood properties, be it blood pressure or sugar etc. Ayurveda of Vedanta determines the abnormality in health of a person by finding out the abnormality of three 'Doshas (Kapha, Pitta, and Vata)'. The symptoms of disease indicate which of the Doshas have increased or decreased and corrective action is taken accordingly.

1.5 Devas (Gods/Goddesses/Deities) in Hinduism

During pre-Vedantic age (prior to 1500 BC), or Vedic age, the religion was somewhat orthodox and there were fewer Gods, such as Indra, Agni, Soma, Varuna, Maruts, Rudra, Vayu and Surya (Aditya) etc. But, after the Aryan invasion/migration, the Vedic people became minority and, as such, Vedic people had to assimilate the gods and cults of the then natives (including Aryans) into their own religion in order to increase their acceptability with the natives. The Puranas represent a religion that is sort of amalgamation of deities from Vedic and native cultures to bring a sort of equilibrium between the two. Many old deities were lost, while new, strange gods with their own mythologies took their place.

Because of Vedanta writings, people understood that faith was an expression of personal freedom, and one could believe at will. That's why Hinduism saw an explosion of Gods. There emerged a God for every need and every creed. Everywhere, divinity appeared in the manner and form we wanted it to appear, and, sometime, when its use was over, we quietly discarded that form of divinity and looked at new forms of the divine that was currently of use to us. Many Hindus see the variety of Gods as figurative representations of aspects of 'One Divinity'. God is so huge that we cannot comprehend God from our limited perspective in human embodiment and so we have all the different Gods to show different sides and aspects of the One. Some believe that God wanted to experience the variety of life and so he split himself into many parts and our experience of the world is only a play that God is enjoying. God reveals Himself to us through His names. Because of the depth of God's character, He has various names that reflect the many ways He relates to humanity. Though Hinduism appears to be a polytheistic religion, all deities originate from the 'One' and merge in the same 'One'. Tolerance and diversity are in the core of Hinduism.

Though the Supreme Power (God) is one and all and he can't be given any name, for understanding the various facets / functions of God, our ancestors have given three different facets of God, as 'Trimurty', which include 'creator' (Lord Brahma), 'preserver / maintainer (Lord Vishnu) and 'destroyer / assimilator (Lord Shiva). Each of these three Lords have their female consort (Saraswathi, Lakshmi & Parvati respectively) to make them complete as per Masculine Energy- Feminine Energy Concept (Sec. 1.3.1). Parvati commands greater importance, in the name of Shakti and has 9 forms (Nine Durgas) and is also considered as 'Adi-Shakti' (the Supreme Being goddess). Each of the three Lords with their consorts and 'Shakti' can collectively be said as 'Super Deities'. The Super Deities produced / created many Gods / Goddesses / deities by way of birth, descendancy, 'Avatars', incarnations or creation by other means, mainly for some specific purposes and they retained their divinity since then. We would discuss them in some detail in subsequent chapters.

Many heavenly bodies are also considered as Gods / deities for their specific functions, such as Sun as Lord Surya, Moon as Lord Chandra, Mars as Lord Mangal, Mercury as Lord Buddha (not Gautam Budhha), Jupitar as Lord Brihaspati (Devaguru, also, sometime, identified as Lord Agni), Venus as Lord Shukracharya and Saturn as Lord Shani etc. There are 9 such heavenly bodies (7 mentioned above plus Rahu and Ketu) which are called Navagraha. As per Vedic / Hindu Astrology, these planets (Navagraha) are relay stations for the reception and transmission of stellar energies. Similarly, Earth, air, water etc. are considered with divine respect.

Another way of classifying Hindu Deities is Ashta Dikpalas, i.e. eight rulers of directions. Directions play a prominent role in Vedic tradition. Of the eight dikpalas, Indra, Varuna, Kubera and Yama are the rulers of the four main directions, namely east, west, north and south respectively. Agni, Niruthi, Isana and Vayu are the rulers of intermediary directions, namely south-east, south-west, north-east and north-west respectively.

Scriptures also say that various devata / demigods (Karma Devas) are actually posts of control, and not individual eternal entities. They (Karma Devas) become residents of heavenly planets by virtue of their good birth and their 'punyas' (pious results) they have accumulated on their earthly realm. Their stay in heaven depends on the amount of their accumulated punya. As they enjoy in the heavenly abode, they use up their punyas and eventually they again fall down to the earthly planet when all punyas used-up.

In Hinduism, there are no typical regular services like in churches & mosques. The Indian temples are not merely prayer halls but quantum healing centers. Temples are, generally, located at places of high Earth energy (magnetic & electromagnetic). We often use copper idols and vessels etc., just to capture that Earth energy. We elevated the status of even a stone to divinity and we could see divinity in it. In most cases, temple architecture is a highly developed science, which also considers divine aspects, energy center of temple, location and shape of deities, metal plates beneath the statues, divine auras, temple bells and conch, space for camphor and parikrama etc. Hindus go to temples whenever they like and visit most of the Gods / deities there. Normally each temple has more than one shrine (murti). People may sit, bend or prostrate in front of the murti, they may also walk in a clockwise circle around it, or meditate in front of it. Most Hindus also have a shrine at home, either in their own room or in a small cabinet built for that purpose. While we worship, God is not bothered about our flower, nivedyam, lamp, mantra, pooja or temple. They are all for our-selves. So, all worship of the God, prayer, mantra, pooja, etc., is for our-selves. Again, 'Homa' (ritual fire, i.e. God Agni) is important in Hinduism. All offerings/prayers etc. are made through the medium of Agni, the great purifier, who alone can purify the offering, so it is worthy of conveying to the deity. Of-course, the sound of temple bells, homa fire and reciting of mantras etc. help two-ways-- one, it helps in concentrating our mind towards our worship and second, it breaks the diseased energies around the area.

1.5.1   Concept of 33 Crores Gods

That we have 33 crores of Gods / deities, is our misunderstanding of fact. We can't even find so many names. Following are the reason for this misunderstanding –

1- Vedas mention 33 Deities / Devas (12 Adityas + 11 Rudras + 8 Vasus + 2 others- some say two Asvins - twin solar Deities, some other say the two are Prajapati and Indra). In Sanskrit, the word 'Koti' has two meanings, one 'the class or type' and another 'the number one crore (10 millions). Vedas meant 33 classes / types of Deities, but we misunderstood that as 33 crores of Deities.

2- Another way to consider 33 Crore Gods is that Hinduism promotes seeing God in all living being, i.e. God is within everyone, accompanying the jivatma (individual soul) as the paramatma (Super-soul). As such, sometime during Vedic Era, when this concept arose, the population of the world was actually about 330 million (33 crores). Considering each individual as a God in his own way (Ahaṁ Brahmāsmīti), it can also be said

that there were 33 crores Gods at that time. The word
'33 Crore Gods' continues even though the population
of world has increased much.

1.5.2   Gods/deities with animal faces

This is the magnanimity of Hinduism. Hanuman (in monkey
form) and Ganesha (with elephant head) are the most revered
and worshipped Gods, barring Vishnu, Shiva and Shakti. There
are many other deities / devas in Hinduism, which are either in
full animal form or part animal form such as Nandi, Varuna,
Kamadhenu, Jambavan, the Nagas, the vahanas (animal mounts
of the Gods) and four of Vishnu's ten incarnations (fish, turtle,
boar and half-man-half-lion) etc. Gods with multiple limbs have
some purpose. They can destroy the sins and punish the sinners,
bless devotees, and provide boons to those who seek them - all
at the same time. Such distinct personalities and forms are based
on how they have been seen in visions and how they are
depicted in stories and legends. There is much imaginative
prowess in such Hindu deities' portrayal. Such deities / devas
illustrate one important aspect of Hinduism that it loves and
respects animals and other creatures or even trees as much as
human being. Such animal deities also propagate the basic Hindu
philosophy that God is in everything and everything (every
saakaar form) is God or part of God (Brahman), i.e. man or
animal or plant or anything, is equal to God. We, thus, see the
Divinity within all living beings and how everyone is a part of
the Supreme in spiritual quality. Such an awareness and
perception increase our respect and concern for all living
creatures.

We can consider this aspect from yet another angle. It is said
that to know what pain is, one has to experience it. As such, to
know the pain of animals, God manifested Himself in animals
and went through their sufferings and pain. Lord Krishna had
said in Bhagavad-Gita, "I manifest in all living beings. I manifest
as Kamdhenu (cow), among trees I am the Peepal tree and
among birds I am the Eagle. That is why, I don't differentiate
between living beings and I treat everyone equally, and so not

partial towards anyone". So, we worship all living beings, including trees and also Water, Air, Fire, Sky and Earth, since these 5 elements too are created by God. Apart from divinity, there are many sacred animals in Hinduism, e.g. cow, elephants, monkeys, tigers and cobras etc. Of-course, divinities with animal attributes are also seen in few other cultures. Worshipping ancestors, saints and seers are also practiced in Hinduism, though in limited scale.

Thus, Hindus worship literally everything. Hindus venerate the entire creation as one and many, acknowledging not only its diversity and duality but also its unity. This approach justifies the fundamental belief of Hinduism that one can reach God through any deity and any path one chooses, as long as the goal is to reach Brahman only or the supreme reality.

1.6   Scriptures in Hinduism

No other living tradition has scriptures as numerous and as ancient as Hinduism, that too with an unbroken chain / practices of faithfully preserved Hindu tradition. Hinduism is not derived from any single book or single person, but it has many sacred writings and oral traditions which serve as a source of doctrine. Scriptures of Hinduism may be classified into two divisions--- "Sruti" (that which is heard) and "Smriti" (that which is remembered) scriptures. Rough classification of scriptures is shown in Fig.1.5.

Vedas (Shruti tradition) are the most ancient and most important scriptures. The Vedas are not considered the works of the human mind but are utterances of what has been realized through intuitive perception by Vedic rishis, who had powers to see beyond the physical phenomena. As such, Vedas may be considered of divine origin. Rig Veda was the first one and taking cue from that, Yajur, Sama & Atharva Vedas came into being. Each of the four Vedas consists of four parts: Samhitas, Brahmanas, Aranyakas, and Upanishads. Sruti and Smriti are also called 'Primary' and 'Secondary' scriptures respectively.

Smriti scriptures are derived from the Vedas but are considered to be of human origin and not of divine origin. They were written to explain and elaborate the Vedas, making them understandable and more meaningful to the general population. The Smrti literature is a vast corpus of diverse texts as shown in Fig.1.5. Most of these, along with many Upanishads can also be called as Vedanta scriptures. Further discussion on scriptures are beyond the scope of this book.

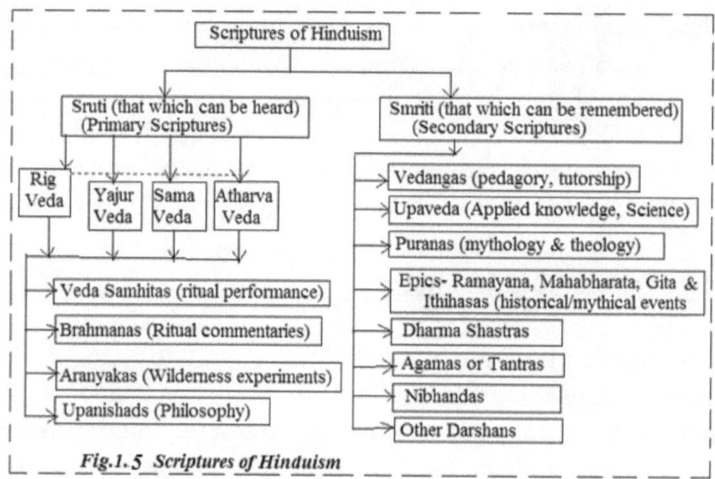

Fig.1.5 Scriptures of Hinduism

1.7   Timeline for Hinduism

Timeline of Hinduism refers to the display of development / evolution of Hinduism in chronological order. Hinduism, including its evolution has already been discussed. Here we have presented the evolution in linear chronological form in Fig. 1.6.

We would discuss very briefly the different eras as per Fig.1.6. The time-period mentioned in the figure are rough, as obtained from various sources.

1- Pre-Vedic Era- Not much is known about pre-Vedic Era except some vague knowledge of Indus Valley Civilization and Harrapan tradition (which is also known as 'Bronze Age of India'). We would consider all period before 1500 BCE as Pre-Vedic. Some go as far back as 8000 BCE.

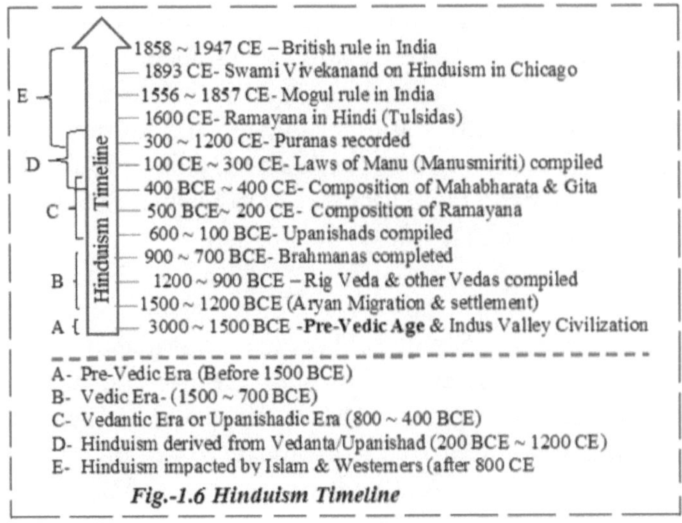

A- Pre-Vedic Era (Before 1500 BCE)
B- Vedic Era- (1500 ~ 700 BCE)
C- Vedantic Era or Upanishadic Era (800 ~ 400 BCE)
D- Hinduism derived from Vedanta/Upanishad (200 BCE ~ 1200 CE)
E- Hinduism impacted by Islam & Westerners (after 800 CE

Fig.-1.6 Hinduism Timeline

2- Vedic Era- The period is taken as 1500 BCE to 700 BCE. Few extend it up-to 500 BCE. It is the period when Aryan migration and settlement took place. It is also the period when Rig Veda and other Vedas and, also, Brahmanas compiled. As it succeeds Harrapan culture, it is also said as Iron-Age of India as some sort of military revolution and warfare started and people developed new and bigger tools, especially after the collapse of Bronze age.

3- Vedantic / Upanishadic Era- The period is taken as 800 BCE to 400 BCE. As people found Vedas rather difficult to understand, they rearranged and simplified the sacred texts in the form of Upanishads, taking the essence / goal of all four Vedas. Ramayana, Mahabharata, Gita and Brahma-sutras were created.

4- Hinduism derived from Vedanta / Upanishad (from 200 BCE ~ 1200 CE)- The word Hinduism didn't find any mention in Pre-Vedic or Vedic Eras. It came into existence in later part of Vedantic Era, taking the gist from Vedas and Upanishads and synthesizing with migrated Aryan traditions and other cultures and traditions of Indian subcontinent at that time. It flourished further post Vedantic Era and Manusmiriti and Puranas etc. were compiled. 'Golden Age' of Hinduism were, probably, Gupta & Pallava period (320 ~ 650 CE) and Classical or Puranic Hinduism was 650 ~ 1200 CE. During these periods, in addition to Indian subcontinent, Hinduism spread to Burma, Siam, Cambodia and up-to south Vietnam.

5- Hinduism impacted by Islam & Westerners (after 800 CE)-Impact of Islam on Hinduism was due to frequent invasions by Arabs and Muslim warlords and subsequent Mogul Rule in India, which led to spread of Islam in India and Hindus had to assimilate few of their traditions in their religion. As Buddhism, Jainism and Sikhism were started by Hindus, Hinduism was further impacted. The subsequent British rule in India also impacted Hinduism. We would not go into good or bad effects of such impacts, except saying that these brought some socio-cultural diffusion and integration in Hinduism and some Hindus got converted to Islam or Christianity.

1.8   Power of prayer in Hinduism

Prayer is an integral part of Hinduism, and for that reason, in most religions. Prayer has been around the longest time in different forms in almost all the cultures, beliefs, faiths and religions of the world. It incorporates a desire within our own body, mind and spirit. It requires specific body movements, mental focus and, also, spiritual interaction within the mind. Prayer increases concentration and helps to pin-point our mind by giving a focal point, be it God, any deity or any other energy source. As said by Alfred Lord Tennyson, 'more things are wrought by prayer than this world can dream off'.

In general, prayers are done in different forms and in different situations for different purposes, but here we would consider the prayers done by us to praise God and to achieve some result or benefit for us, be it our health or others. Science, now, agrees that there is a relaxation response the body goes to when people pray and mediate. The heart rate slows, and blood pressure also goes down as the body goes into a calming state. Prayer also brings a synchronized, harmonious and intelligent interaction of minds, scientifically directed for a specific purpose.

Prayers have many other benefits, c.g. it gives us a more positive outlook, combating depression and reducing the risk of developing depression, it improves immune system and can reduce asthma symptoms and it gives sense of well-being, which leads to longer life.

In prayer, we consciously choose a certain idea / plan that we want to experience or achieve and a mental picture of our desired deity and convey that idea or mental picture to our mind and having faith for achieving that. The 'art' of prayer is our technique or process and the 'science' of the prayer is the knowledge and the definite purpose of the mind to our mental picture or thought. Any prayer should have, in addition to other aspects, following approaches / components-

1- Sincerity of desire and purpose,
2- Vision and mental picture of purpose,
3- Focused and relaxed mind,
4- Muster attention and focus on thought of solution,
5- Repetition of pledge and affirmation of purpose. Of-course it succeeds only when it is specific and does not produce any mental conflict or arguments,
6- Thanking the deity or the Almighty. A thankful mind and heart are always, close creative forces. As such we must thank the Almighty (or our preferred deity) at least at the start and end of prayer.

1.8.1   Modus Operandi of prayer

God or preferred deity doesn't come to give us our desired results but prepares us mentally to achieve those. Many methods can be said for modus operandi of prayer, but here we would limit to the following three main methods, as to how the prayer works. However, we should avoid all undue efforts and coercion in prayer.

1- By entrusting our worries to God-- While praying, we entrust / repose all our worries or other negative emotions / feeling to God, Almighty, any preferred deity. After entrusting our worries etc., we become mentally free of those and we can concentrate all our energies for achievement of our desired result or betterment of our life. By the very feeling that God will take care of all our worries and problems, we will have no inhibition or fear of not achieving our goal.

2- By Lifting of consciousness & alertness- The simple belief that the God (or any preferred deity) is all bliss, boundless love and wisdom, infinite intelligence, absolute harmony and all powerful and always ready to help us for right cause, our consciousness and alertness are lifted up into a new spiritual wavelength. To the extent we rise in our consciousness by contemplating qualities and attributes of God, to the similar extent the spiritual electronic waves of harmony and peace are generated within us, which, in-turn, dissolve all our problems / worries. When we realize that the power that moves and the world is moving on our behalf and is backing up on our words / desires, our confidence and assurance grows.

3- Increase in Thought Force Intensity- In this world, everything throws-off some emanations / vibrations. Be it electric stove, flower or musk and mobile phone, they all throw some emanation/vibration which we call as heat, odor or electromagnetic waves, though we may not see those. Similarly, when a person is thinking, his/her mind throws off emanations, which usually becomes thinner and less easily perceived as it extends away from the sender. These emanations are called 'Thought

Waves'. Again, if a small particle of musk is exposed in a room and then removed, and yet the odor will be perceptible for some time. In the same way, when a person thinks, the generated thought waves remains for some time and dies gradually. Again, more sincerely and seriously a person thinks, stronger will be the generated thought waves. During prayer, the person thinks seriously and repeatedly about the God and the purpose and, as such, the generated thought waves becomes stronger and stronger and becomes a 'Though Force'. To the extent the intensity of such thought force increases, our mind will automatically work more effectively for achieving the results. For further details about thought waves, thought force and their effect on prayer, the reader may refer to author's earlier book, "Healing by Reprogramming of Instinctive Mind", given in bibliography.

1.9   Influence of Hinduism in Hollywood Movies

It is logical that Hinduism has enormous influence on Bollywood and other Indian movies and, as such, we are not discussing it here. But Hinduism has enough influence on Hollywood movies also, and we shall discuss that very briefly. The philosophy behind quite a few Hollywood super hit movies is based on Hinduism. Apparent and hidden references to Hindu symbolism can be found in many movies, including Batman, Superman and Memento. Just for example, we would examine the plots of following three movies that are based on Vedic teachings.

1- Avatar (year 2009) - The term 'Avatar' is most widely associated in Hinduism with Lord Vishnu, whose Avatars (incarnations) are often depicted as having blue skin (e.g. Lord Krishna or Lord Rama), similar to the actor Na'vi in movie Avatar. Just like Vishnu, takes avatars and descends to save the order of the universe, the film's 'avatar' also descends to avert impending ultimate doom, effected by a rapacious greed that leads to destroying the world. In Hinduism, there is a concept called 'Parakaya Pravesham' in which a person leaves one's body temporarily and enters the body of another person. There are many stories of demigods and few demons entering the body of others temporarily. Even Sri Adi Sankara had also entered the body of King Amaruka of Benares (now Varanasi) temporarily. Something similar happens in the movie Avater as humans are able to temporarily enter the body of a Na'vi, or vise-versa. Yet another similarity is that the characters in movie Avatar rides on a flying dragon like being. This is more like Lord Vishnu riding on a giant bird Garuda or other Indian deities are shown flying on a bird/animal cum vehicle.

2- Matrix Trilogy (years 1999~2003)- Peter Rader, producer of movie Matrix, said that the Matrix movie is, actually, based on yogic and Vedic principles. It says that this world is an illusion. It's 'Maya', made by God to hide himself to all people. If we can cut through the illusions and connect with something larger (say God or other deity), we can do all sorts of things. The hero of the movie gains the capabilities of advanced Yogis who are believed to be able to defy laws of normal reality. The concept of "Guru" or spiritual teacher is admirably shown through the interaction of Morpheus and Neo. The action choreography of the movies especially of that between Neo and Mr. Smith at the end, matches the descriptions of fighting between Duryodhana and Bhima in the Mahabharata.

3- Interstellar (year 2014)- The total plot design of this movie was based on the ideal of a universal super-consciousness that transcends space and time and in which all human life is connected. This belief has actually existed for nearly 3000 years and the concept itself originates from the Vedic period. In this movie, there is a concept-- 1 Hour on Miller planet is equal to 7 Years on Earth. Due to a technical problem, the team is forced to spend 3 hours on that planet resulting in the loss of 23 years on Earth. Which means 10 years old daughter of hero becomes 33 years old and the hero remains of the same age. This is just like Gita giving a story that king Kakudmi and his daughter Revati traveled through heaven to meet Lord Brahma. Lord Brahma explained them that time runs differently on different planes of existence, and that during the short time they had waited in heaven to see him, thousands of years had passed on Earth. When King Kakudmi and Revati returned to earth, they were shocked by the changes that had taken place. Again, actor McConaughey's character also engages in a situation that refers somewhat Indra's net (also called Indra's jewels or Indra's pearls, or Indrajāla). Indra's Net is a Hindu metaphor that portrays the entire universe as an everlasting "web of existence spun by the king of the gods, each of its intersections adorned with an infinitely sided jewel, everyone continually reflecting the others". The Indra-net concept, later, became the central principle of Buddhism, and from there spread into Western discourses.

Having discussed Hinduism in very brief, we would come to the title of the book, which consists of three simple catch words—'Corporate' (i.e. corporation), 'Governance' and 'Universe', which simply means corporation style governance / management of universe, i.e. the way our universe is being governed or managed appears to be somewhat similar to the management of any big or small corporation/ establishment.

~~~~~~~~~~~~~~~~~~~~~~~~~~~
~~~~~~~~~~~~~~~~~~~~~~~~~~~

2   Universe vis-à-vis Corporation

(I read Hinduism and realized that it is for the religion of all the world and all mankind --- Bertrand Russell, 1872 - 1970)

Before we proceed to discuss the governance/management aspect of universe or corporation, we should discuss briefly what they are or what we mean by them?

2.1   What do we mean by Universe

We can discuss universe in two ways- 'materialistic way' and 'philosophical way' or 'scientific way' and 'Vedic way'. 'Materialistic way' or 'scientific way' considers that the Universe (physical) is all of space and time and their contents, including planets, stars, galaxies, and all other forms of matter and energy. The universe is believed to be at least 10 billion light years in diameter and has been expanding since its creation in the Big Bang about 13 billion years ago. It means that the Universe has neither an edge nor a center.

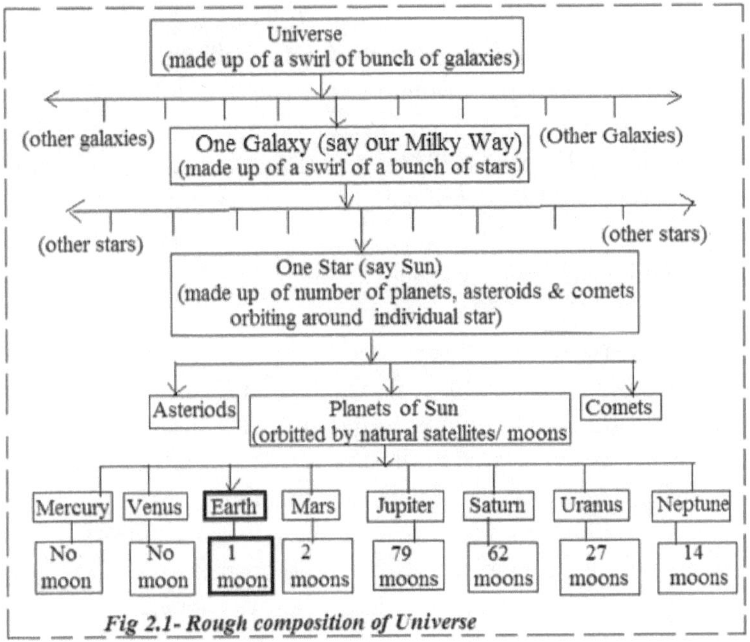

Fig 2.1- Rough composition of Universe

While the spatial size of the entire Universe is still unknown, it is possible to measure the observable universe. The Universe can also be defined as "the totality of existence", or everything that exists, everything that has existed, and everything that will exist". However, one thing is certain, i.e. human beings have existed for only a small fraction of cosmic history. The human race has been improving so rapidly in knowledge and technology that if people had been around for millions of years, the human race would be much further along in its domination.

The rough composition of the Universe is shown in Fig.2.1. In a very simplified way, the Universe is made up of a swirl of cluster / bunch of celestial objects, i.e. galaxies--- each galaxy is made up of a swirl of cluster / bunch of stars, each star has number of its own asteroids, comets and planets (orbiting around its own sun) and most of the planets have number of their own satellites / moons. As a rough estimate, our universe may be having around 80 billion galaxies (large or small, spiral, elliptical or irregular in shape, normal or active, i.e. exploding with vast amount of energy). Our galaxy (Milky Way-- a large and spiral type) may be having 200 ~ 400 billion stars. Many of the stars may be called 'red dwarves', i.e. small, faint and red in color. The universe may contain very many Earth like planet which may sustain life in some form or other. In the figure, we have highlighted our own planet (Earth) and its moon. We have considered only 8 planets of sun, excluding Pluto.

2.1.1   Universe vis-à-vis space

Often the two terms, 'space' and 'universe' are used synonymously by some, but there is distinct difference between the two. Space, also known as 'outer space', is the void that exists between all celestial bodies. It consists of a hard vacuum comprising a low density of particles, mainly a plasma of hydrogen and helium. It may also include magnetic fields, electromagnetic radiation, neutrinos and cosmic rays. The Universe is all the matter and energy that was generated / released by the Big Bang. The key difference between the two terms is that Universe includes all the space and all the celestial objects. Thus, the Universe is a sort of a bubble with a radius of over 10 billion light years. The 'outer space' is the part of the Universe that's outside of Earth's atmosphere. Earth is part of the Universe, but, by definition, is not part of outer space. Intergalactic space (space between galaxies) takes up most of the volume of the Universe. In most galaxies, 90% of the mass is in an unknown form called dark matter, which interacts with other matter through gravitational forces.

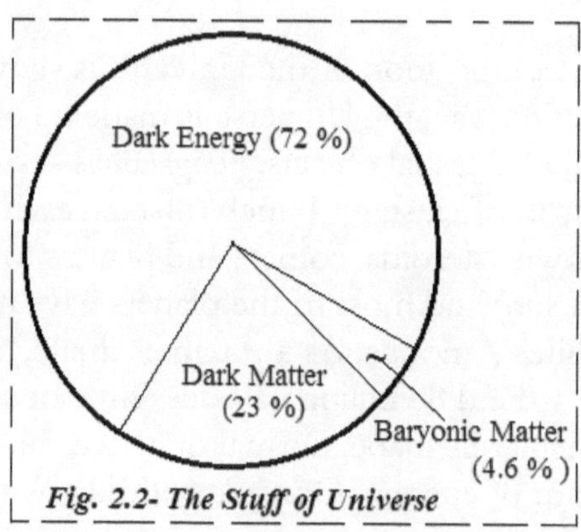

Fig. 2.2- The Stuff of Universe

As per one of the posting of NASA, Fig.2.2 roughly shows what the universe is made of. All the galaxies and their stuff are termed as 'Baryonic matter' (about 4.6%) and rest are 'Dark Energy' (72 %) and 'Dark Matter' (23%). The figure, of-course, doesn't account for 0.4%. To avoid confusion, we may consider Baryonic matter as 5%. This includes the smallest components atomic particles followed by atoms (mostly free hydrogen and helium), molecules, dust, space rocks, comets, asteroids, moons, dwarf planets, planets, solar systems, stars, black holes, nebulae, and galaxies etc. In simple term, Dark matter is composed of particles that do not absorb, reflect, or emit light, so they cannot be detected by observing electromagnetic radiation or other known means. It interacts predominantly via gravity with visible matter (e.g., Baryonic Matter). Dark energy is the name given to the unknown force that is believed to be making the universe larger. Thus, the Dark matter produces an attractive force (gravity), while dark energy produces a repulsive force (antigravity).

2.1.2   Vedic Approach vis-à-vis Modern Science

The study of universe from Vedic angle (including philosophical way) is very complex but less understood. While modern science gives us volumes of information about universe, the whole picture of life is missing, and we lack wisdom that allows us to see the source of everything. Max Planck (of quantum theory fame) said that there is a conscious intelligent spirit behind the universe. This is similar to the view of our saints who said that there is a conscious power which has drawn the plan of life.

As per Vedas, the cosmic energy first entered through the cosmic word "Shabd Brahma" or "Nada brahmin" (also known as 'OM' pronounced as 'AUM'), which changed into mass as Hiranyagarbha (the cosmic 'golden Egg' or 'golden womb'), also known as 'Brahma Egg' or 'Brahmanda'. Some scripture says that wishing to create the universe, Brahman, the Supreme Power, first created the water, in which he placed his seed. This seed transformed into a golden egg, from which Brahma appeared. For this reason, Brahma is also known as 'Hiranyagarbha'. On the opening or bursting of this "Brahma Egg" great mass of this entire universe was formed with the combination of subtle Gunas (quality of mind) in different proportions, along with subtle and gross particles, atoms / molecules etc. Many others say that when Brahman wished to create the Universe, He made Brahma to come out from His naval, sitting on a lotus and within the stem of lotus are the 14 Planetary system. Brahma, then, taking ingredients and elements from infinite resources of Brahman, created the universe, the entire universe visible to human eye, perceivable by senses, visualized by scientists with powerful telescopes and other instruments along with non-visible subtle worlds. Considering Multi- universe (Multiverse), different Brahma will appear for each Universe. Brahma is also known as Svayambhu (self-born) and Vagisa (Lord of Speech). As per Vedas only about one fourth (1/4) of the entire Brahmand is visible and remaining are Brahmaloka, Deva loka, Swarga etc., which no material eye, senses or instruments can see except the human manifested soul.

Vedic scriptures also say that the supreme Lord Brahman (say Maha-Vishnu or Sada-Shiva) is the whole universe, which is divided into fourteen planetary systems. Seven planetary systems (also called Lokas)--- known as Bhur (Earth or Mrityu Lok), Bhuvar (Geospace- abode of siddhas / spirits, near to Earth, but between Earth & Heaven), Svar (say Solar system), Mahar (say the world of stars), Janas (say the Milky Way Galaxy), Tapas (say the world of Galaxies) and Satya (say the Universe)--- are upward planetary systems, one above the other and there are also seven planetary systems downward, known as Atala, Vitala, Sutala, Talātala, Mahātala, Rasātala and Pātāla, gradually, one below the other (which are supposed to be located at different levels below the top crust of earth and supposed to be hotter and not easy to live for normal human) and all of these are situated in the various parts of the Lord's body. The lower planetary systems, starting from bottom up-to Bhur Lok are said to be situated in his legs. The middle planetary systems, beginning from Bhuvarloka, are situated in his navel. And the still higher planetary systems, occupied by the demigods and highly cultured sages and saints, are situated in the chest of the Supreme Lord. All these planetary systems (Lokas) are scattered over the complete universe, which are still the parts of supreme Lord's body.

The first half of famous 'Gayatri Mantra' (om̐ bhur bhuvaḥ svaḥ tat savitur vareṇyam) says that above the Bhuloka (Earth or Prithvi) planetary system is Bhuvarloka and above that is Swargaloka, the heavenly planetary system and all these planetary systems are controlled by Savitā, the sun-god. For common people all these planetary systems are grouped in three planetary systems— upper, middle and lower. Those influenced by the mode of goodness (Akarma or Nishkam Karma) are given places in the upper planetary systems (say Swarga Loka) which include all above Bhuvar Loka). Those influenced by the mode of passion are given places in middle planetary system (say Bhulok which includes Bhurloka and Bhuvarloka). Those influenced by the mode of ignorance and sin (Vikarma) are given places in lower planetary system (say Narak Lok, i.e. Hell) which includes Atāla, Vitāla, Sutāla, Talātala, Mahātala, Rasātala, Pātāla.

Apparently, the conception of cosmos (Universe) between Vedic approach and modern science approach differs much, but, actually, the difference is not much. Scientists from University of South Denmark and some others have warned that the universe may, one day, collapse and everything in it, including Earth, will be compressed into a small superhot ball (so called Big-crunch). But the Vedas and Upanishads go much beyond. They say that Lord Brahma (or the Supreme Lord) created the universe in its present form and the universe will, one day, end into a state of subtle point and will get merged / submerged into that Supreme Lord. That will be one 'Cosmic Cycle'. After the end of the cosmic cycle, there will be absolutely nothing, except the Supreme Lord (Brahman). The Supreme Lord will again create a new universe to start a new cosmic cycle and, thus the creation of cosmic cycles goes on.

As another disparity with Vedic approach, few scientists say that Vedic approach (Puranas) shows Earth as flat surface. This is, some sort of misunderstanding by them. Fig.2.3 shows the universe as Brahmanda. In the center, a disc shaped Earth, called 'Bhu-Mandala' is shown. This may be considered as polar (azimuthal) projection of the near spherical Earth. Few scientists have opined that the so-called flat Earth of ancient times originally represented the plane of the ecliptic (the orbit of the sun) and not the Earth on which we stand (Fig.2.4) and which was later taken by some as flat earth. Few opined that Bhu-mandala was also intended to represent the realm of the devas. As shown in Fig 2.3, this Bhu-mandla divides the Brahmanda in upper heavenly half (consisting the six Lokas above the Bhur Loka) and the lower subterranean half, filled with water and the seven Lokas below the Bhur Loka supposed to be in that. The Bhu-Mandala has many Islands and oceans and in the center is the Jambudvipa. The total may be considered as Bharata-varsha, which can be understood in one sense as India and in another as the total area inhabited by human beings. The figure presents an earth-centered conception of the cosmos / universe.

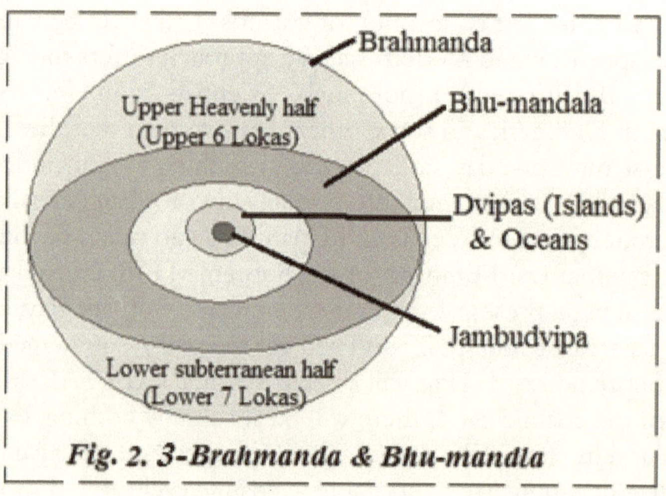

Fig. 2. 3-Brahmanda & Bhu-mandla

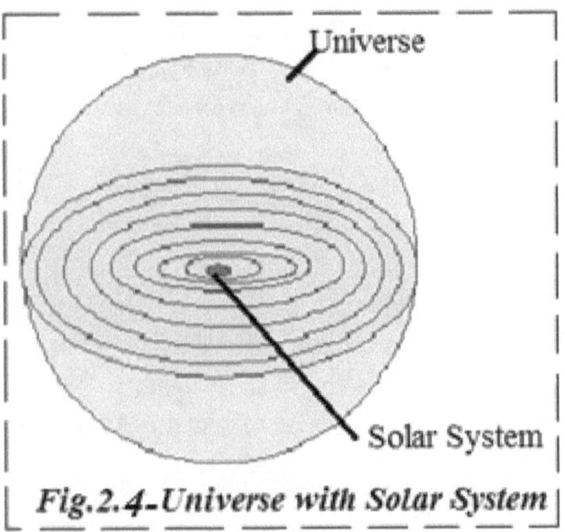

Fig.2.4-Universe with Solar System

2.1.3   Transformation of Brahman into Universe

Brahman transformed itself into the 'Obvious Universe' at three levels of manifestation. The first is the Super-subtle state (Casual state) called Iswara (the supreme power, i.e. Brahman endowed with Maya or illusion). The second stage (subtle stage) is the Mental level called Hiranyagarbha (golden womb, which is the source of the creation of the whole Universe or cosmos). Then, after creation of the 'Pancha Tanmatra' (5 perceptions- i.e. form/touch, smell, taste, sound & sight) and 'Pancha Bhutas' (5 elements- Earth, water, fire, sky / ether & air) etc., the third stage. i.e. the Physical level called Virat or Viswa (gross world) was created. All of us, humans, animals, plants, rocks and other materials are part of this structure and so the same three levels are present in all of us. This aspect would be discussed further in chapter-4.

Considering 'Ahaṁ Brahmāsmīti' in the human, at the Super-subtle level, it is called the Jiva or Jivatma or Soul, at the Mental level, it is called the Mind and at the Physical level it is called the Body. In Vedanta, these levels in the human being are also called Pragna (or Sushupti), Taijasa (or Swapna) and Vaiswanara (or Jagruta), which correspond respectively to the Deep sleep, the

Dreaming and the Waking states in humans. They also correspond to the Suvaha, the Bhuvar and Bhu Lokas and to the 'M', 'U' and 'A' sounds of the 'AUM or Omkara' respectively.

2.1.4   I am the Universe

Few modern scientists / philosophers, sometime, raise a concept of 'I am the Universe' or 'You are the Universe' or 'We are the Universe'. In this context, the Vedic / Hindu philosophy (Adi Shankaracharya) has already said, "Ahaṁ Brahmāsmīti" which means, "I am the God" or "I am the Absolute". This has been discussed briefly in Sec.1.3, Sec.1.3.2 and Sec.2.1.3.

Few modern scientists / philosophers say that the universe exists, because there is consciousness of the universe. This also means that consciousness must have come first, creating a quantum jump from singularity to duality. Cosmic consciousness operates thru separate events, which are too far apart to be considered in touch with each other, but at the same time, it holds these events together, at a deeper level, where nothing is separate.

The building block of universe is "Qualia", i.e. five natural senses plus 'sensation', 'image', 'feeling' and 'thought'. However, pure consciousness has no "Qualia"—it is the source of "Qualia". Consciousness makes all experience possible. Every specific form of consciousness (a person, an elephant or a snake or an insect) experiences the world subjectively, but the individual subjectivity remains within the field of consciousness. Pure consciousness give rise to everything, including human mind. The universe may have become conscious of itself and we live in cosmic universe and we are a cosmic self. We participate in the same consciousness that is the universe. Thus, the phrase "I am the Universe" comes from the realization that you're not separate from any of it and never could be no matter how hard you tried. Refer also to Sec.4.6.3.

2.1.5   Universe vis-à-vis World

Universe and world are two words that we sometimes used interchangeably. However, these two words carry different meanings and can't be used interchangeably on most occasions. World generally refers to the Earth, together with all people and countries along with human's and other living being's civilization. Universe refers to solar systems, planets, moons, stars, and the contents of intergalactic space, all matter and energy considered as a whole. Thus, the world is a part of the universe. World is, also, called 'Physical Universe'. However, in cosmology, world can refer to any planet, such as Mars, Saturn, Jupiter or Earth.

2.2   What is Corporation and Corporate Governance

A corporation is a company or group of people or an organization authorized to act as a single entity and recognized as such in law. It is a legal entity that is separate and distinct from its owners. Corporations may be of different structures such as Sole Proprietorship, General Partnership, Limited Partnership and Limited Liability Companies etc. Again, though the main purpose of corporation may be maximizing shareholder value, corporations can be for different purposes, e.g. Business Corporation, Municipal Corporation, Cooperative Corporation, Professional Corporation, Non-profit Corporation, a sport club, or a government of a new city or town etc. Corporations can also be classified in the manner its profits are taxed or number of shareholders and stocks to be issued. A nonprofit corporation is an organization that uses surplus or given revenues to achieve its goals rather than distributing them as profit or dividends. It may also be in the form of 'charities' or 'foundations'.
A municipal corporation of a city, town, or village has governmental powers. The day-to-day activities of a corporation are typically controlled by individuals appointed by the members. In smaller corporations, this may be a single individual, but more commonly, corporations are controlled by a committee. Corporation's structure consists of various departments and

divisions that contribute to the company's overall mission and goals.

We thus see that the scope of corporation is very vast. For the purpose of this book, we can consider the whole universe as a corporation, with the Supreme Power (Brahman) at the top, supervising his three faces, Brahma, Vishnu and Shiva as chiefs (Managing Director) of three main division of Universe, i.e. creation, preservation and dissolution. More about this later.

Governance of any corporation should have vision, mission and objectives and strategy to achieve those. The total governance functions can be classified in two broad categories-policies and procedures. For a big corporation, policies are decided by corporate or central office and procedures are the responsibility of individual establishments. Figure 2.5 shows the broad functions of each, which are self-explanatory. For smaller corporations, the total functions may be considered by the same establishment. For our further discussions, we would consider all included in corporate governance / management.

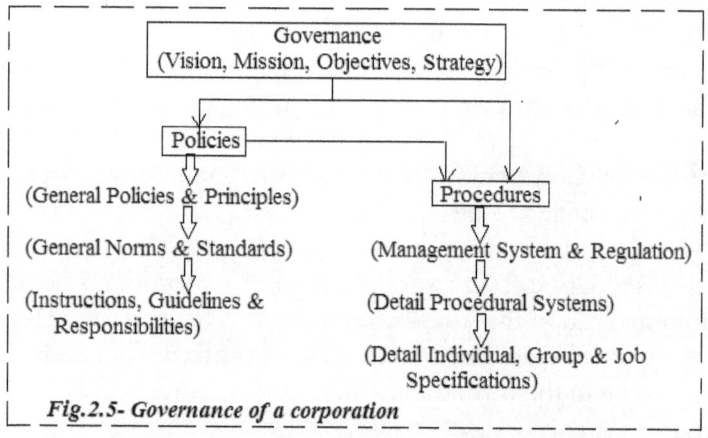

Fig.2.5- Governance of a corporation

Corporate governance / management refers to all levels of managerial personnel and executives in a business or any such entity that has been incorporated. Informally, corporate management may refer to managers and executives that operate at the corporate headquarters and act as the primary leaders of the business or that entity. Such managerial roles may be found in human resources, information technology, production, finance, legal, healthcare and other executive areas. Corporate governance / management is responsible to formulate specific and simple policies to be follow by all concerned, yet the policies should have some flexibility so that they can be applied to the various sections (may be at different locations) of that business / entity. It also calls for connecting and coordinating various portions of that business entity through communication, meetings and other organized processes.

Two types of decision-making styles are found in corporate governance / management: centralized and decentralized structures. Centralized decision making involves from top to bottom in making decision, but the decentralized styles delegate decision-making authority to managers at each division and department level, considering the given corporate mission / goal. Choosing a style depends on the size and security aspects of business / entity. Considering the universe as a corporation, the decentralized style appears to be working.

2.2.1   Corporate Management vis-à-vis Governance

Experts differentiate between 'corporate management' and 'corporate governance'. Basically, governance is primarily about protecting a business or any entity, while management is more about growing it. Governance refers to the policies and procedures set in place to ensure a business or entity operates within the law and for the optimal benefit of all stakeholders. Management refers to the techniques the executives and other concerned personnel use to help the company / entity operate and flourish. Governance, sometime, refers to policies that specifically restrict or direct how people can act. Many governance policies pertain to financial activities, setting procedures for soliciting and awarding contracts, accounting practices, disbursing profits and providing transparency for shareholders. Management refers to the actions taken by a company to lead the business in a positive direction. Analyses of operations help management to determine if the company needs to change any practices, such as bringing contracted work in-house or vice versa, setting new goals, modifying the market mix and monitoring financial performance. However, the two terms often overlap in actual working and, as such, we would consider both in the term 'corporate governance'. It takes care of policy formation, resource utilization, finance, coordination, control, staffing, communication, performance appraisal, training and development of staff and technological development etc. Somewhat similar corporate governance seems to be working for the universe.

2.3   Constituents of Universe and Corporation

This section may be considered as extension of Sec.2.1 and Sec. 2.2. As per Rene Descartes, the Universe consists of two kind of substances; first 'matter' which is described as 'extended substance' and includes all the physical stuff like galaxies, radiations, dark matter, dark energy etc. and all the biological stuff and second 'mind/ consciousness' which can be described as 'thinking substance' and includes all the mental and psychological states / issues. Again, as per Greek philosopher, Pluto, the universe is a gigantic living organism. But these appear rather complex for common people. So, we have broken down the constituents / ingredients of universe in Table T-2.1. Two specialties of living beings are that they reproduce and adapt to their environments. Non-living things are those which were once alive (coal) or have never been alive (stone). They can be natural or man-made. The living parts of an ecosystem are called biotic factors and the nonliving parts are called abiotic factors. Mixed may include two types--- one, which are actually non-living but work somewhat as living (modern robots) or second- those who are really half dead or half alive. Otherwise, the table is self-explanatory.

Table- T-2.1, Constituents of Universe

Categories	Constituents
Living	All human beings, animals, fishes, birds, flies, bees, Extra-Terrestrials, all other creatures, trees, algae, fungi, beetles,

	sponges, jellyfish, reptiles, condors, bacteria and all other living organisms.
Non-living	Rocks, soil, water, snow, clouds, air, other gasses, woods, minerals, metallic and non-metallic ores, dead shells and man-made items like buildings, machines, furniture etc.
Mixed	Not too late dead animals, plants and mosses etc.
Galactic & other celestial objects	All galaxies, black holes, quasars, stars, nebulae, planets (some of which includes us, living & non-living), asteroids, comets, moons etc.
Cosmic Rays, Radiations & Microwaves.	All the gravitational force, magnetic and nuclear fields, electromagnetic radiation, neutrinos, and other cosmic rays.
Supernatural	All Devas, demi-gods, angels, rishis & super saints, souls & spirits, veils, ghosts, demons, monsters etc. (mostly non-physical entities, which are not clearly understood by us)
Laws & others	Various laws and all those, not covered in above six categories

Similarly, for understanding of commoners, we have broken down the constituents / ingredients of a corporation in Table T-2.2, which, again, is self-explanatory. These two tables show the similarity in understanding of universe and a corporation and help us in understanding the corporate governance of the universe.

Table- T-2.2- Constituents of Corporation

Categories	Constituents
Living	All direct and indirect workmen, technician, executives, advisors, administrative & legal staff, janitors & cleaning staff, packers, transporters, distributors, stockists, buyers, sellers and so on.
Non-living	All raw materials, buildings, offices, furniture, machines and instruments, stationaries, computers and associated hardware and

	software, protecting gadgets, transports & communication devices etc.
Mixed	Artificial Intelligence items e.g. Kuri Home Robots, Robot Dogs, Dashbot AI Robots for cars, AI Robot Companions & other modern robots, Amelia, Google Home, Modern Drones etc.
Energy	All sorts of thermal & geothermal, hydroelectric, solar, nuclear, wind, gravitational, tidal, wave, hydrogen, biomass and fossil fuel energy sources, used in industries and corporations
Internet & Web	All sorts of Internet, Intranet, Internet of Things (IoT), web applications, cloud applications etc.
Ideas, Goals, Mental	Human (and perhaps selective animal) mind is the most important component of any corporation to foresee & set goals, missions, ways & methods etc.
Laws & others	Various laws and all those, not covered in above six categories.

2.4   Challenges of Universe and Corporation

While there may be very many challenges in understanding the governance of universe and governance and management of a corporation, we would pick up only five simple challenges, as given in Table T-2.3, for understanding the comparison between the two.

Table T-2.3- Challenges of Universe and Corporation

Sl.	Challenges in Universe	Challenges in Corporation
1	Universe is expanding far faster than expected, causing huge problem of our understanding. Its rate of expansion does not match predictions based	In big corporation & industries, sometime the initial specifications were underrated, and the actual constraints faced were much more than estimated

	on measurements of the remnant radiation left over from the Big Bang. It may challenge the Einstein's theory of relatively.	at planning stage. This creates big problem and calls for major revisions.
2	Possible massive cosmic collision- Scientists believe that some galactic collision and star bursting have already happened in distant past and may again happen in distant future, even though most of them are far apart to reduce such possibility. If that would involve our Sun or Earth, whole life force may be affected.	Major corporations & industries sometime get devasted either by internal disaster (major fire etc.) or external disaster (earthquakes, volcanic eruptions, tsunami etc.), even though few of such possibilities are considered at planning stage. The corporation may, then, need relocation or major reconstruction.
3	Challenge the universe- Often the universe isn't fair, and things don't work out neatly; pain, hardship and challenges are then divided among those best equipped to deal with them.	Challenge the corporation- Often the corporation may not appear to be fair for few individuals and they may feel pain, hardship or frustration. They have to face the challenges within the corporation, readjusting their and their colleagues' workload and win over the problems.
4	As the universe is so complex, getting a "big picture" of the universe as a whole, is often difficult challenge for both, commoners & professionals	For a big corporation, having multiple activities, multiple products and at different locations, getting a big picture is often challenging for many of us.
5	Merger of galaxies in universe- It is said that about 1.5 billion years after	Merger of different entities-- Mergers and acquisitions (M&A) are

| Big Bang, many young starburst galaxies began colliding and merging in form of massive galaxies. Such megamerger forms a cluster of galaxies, gravitationally bound by dark matter and ultimately settling together into one gigantic galaxy. | common in big industrials & corporations. It means consolidation of companies. Mergers is the combination of two or more companies to form one, while Acquisitions is one company taken over by the other. It improves financial performance & reduces risks. |

2.5   The cycle of Universe vis-à-vis the Corporation

The universe, we are living in, is not a permanent universe. Some scientists have suggested that, following the Big Bang, the process of the expansion of the universe will eventually be reversed and, at some distant point in the future, will start to contract, eventually imploding into a `Big Crunch', when all energy is lost. Thus, one cycle would be Big Bang, expand, collapse and crunch-- that's the end. This may lead to another 'Big Bang', with a new universe being formed. The cycle of 'Big Bang' and then 'Big Crunch' has been termed as 'Big Bounce' by some scientists. This relates to the Vedic concept of present Brahma day coming to an end and to be followed by another Brahma Day.

Based on this hypothesis, Fig. 2.6 shows the scientific approach of the cycle of universe. Considering the present big bang as 'nth cycle and present universe as nth universe, the coming big crunch will be the nth big crunch when the whole universe will finish / vanish. After some time and with some coincidences, the $(n+1)^{th}$ big bang will occur, creating the $(n+1)^{th}$ universe which will, again, finish after $(n+1)^{th}$ big crunch and this cycle will go on. Modern science is yet quite vague about the anticipated durations about these cycles, and so also about the gap between preceding 'Big Crunch' and succeeding 'Big Bang' (x-1 and x-2 in the figure), but Vedic scriptures have given more specific information about such cycles.

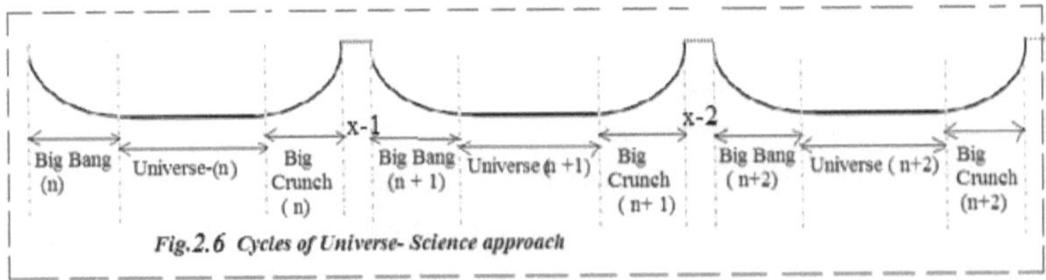

Fig.2.6 Cycles of Universe- Science approach

This is the concept of 'Cycle of universe' or 'Cyclic Universe'. 'Multi-universe' (multiverse) is, another concept as per which very many (may be infinite number) universes existing at the same time, many at different stages of evolution. However, Aristotle, the famous Greek philosophers, and some other philosophers / scientists believed that the universe had existed forever. Something eternal is more perfect than something created. The motivation for believing in an eternal universe was the desire to avoid invoking divine intervention to create the universe and set it going. Contrary to that, those who believed the universe had a beginning, used it as an argument for the existence of God as the prime mover and the supreme power of the universe.

According to Hindu Vedic cosmology, there is no absolute start time, as it is considered infinite and cyclic. The current universe is just the start of a present cycle preceded by an infinite number of universes and to be followed by another infinite number of universes. As per Vedic approach, Maha-Vishnu (or Supreme Power Brahman or Purusha) represents the eternity and is the personification of the eternal multiverse and He, as multi-universe (or Omniverse), exists forever without any beginning or end. This eternal Universe is Self-existent (swayambhu), Self-illuminating (Swayamprakasha), Self-evident (Pratyaksa) and Self-pulsating (Swayam-sphurita). Brahma is the personification of our temporary physical universe that was created by Him (same as the big bang). Brahma is said to have been created from the navel (which is a single point and is symbolized as the root of creation) of Maha-Vishnu (Brahman), described as a lotus blooming out of the navel, much like our big bang universe. Brahma resides inside or on this lotus, creates the universe that we live in and the life form in that. Brahma also represents the universe he has created. A universe endures for about 4.3 billion human years (one day of Brahma or Kalpa). Within each Kalpa (Brahma Day) many Divya Yugs (Chatur Yuga- refer Fig.5.1) occur, which are, often partially devastated (pralaya), by fire or water etc., before start of new Yuga, within the universe. Finally, the whole universe is destroyed/dissolved (Maha- pralaya) at the end of Brahma Day and then Brahma rests for one night, just as long as the day. Some say that Brahma, at the end of His day, goes back inside the navel of Maha-Vishnu (Brahman) for His night and comes out again after that to create fresh universe. This process goes on forever and is shown in Fig.2.7.

This time cycle is also called as Kaala Chakra - the Wheel of Time (Alchemy Wheel). Here Brahma is somewhat synonymous to mass as Hiranyagarbha, golden Egg, golden womb or 'Brahma Egg' mentioned in Sec.2.1.2.

As per Shaiva scriptures, at first the ultimate truth "Brahman" was Shiva without any birth or death. Vishnu is formed from the Vaamanga of Shiva or the left body. However, it is Brahman--- we may call Vishnu or Shiva.

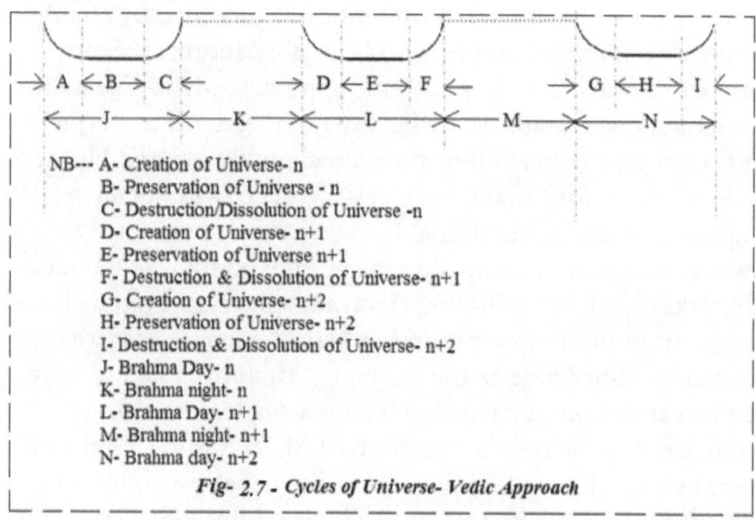

Fig- 2.7 - Cycles of Universe- Vedic Approach

Corporation and industries also have three stages--- Creation (also known as start-up stage), Running & Upkeep (including initial growth stage and later maturity stage) and dissolution (including decline and death / disposal stages). Reasons of dissolution may be obsolescence of end-product or raw material, partnership disagreement, losses etc. These three stages make one cycle of the corporate entity / industry. Sometime after dissolution, another corporate entity may start at the same place or nearby, taking some advantage of leftover material or resources. Say after the dissolution of a steel plant lot of slag was leftover / dumped nearby and considering those slag as possible raw material, a cement plant may start there or nearby. Thus, the next life cycle, in the form of next corporate entity will start. After the dissolution of cement plant, may be some other entity come up, either a completely new version for same or similar product or for altogether different product. This cycle of corporate entity is shown in Fig.2.8, starting with corporate entity no. 'n'. The periods between dissolution of previous entity and creation of next entity (x-1 and x-2 in the figure) can't be foreseen much in advance.

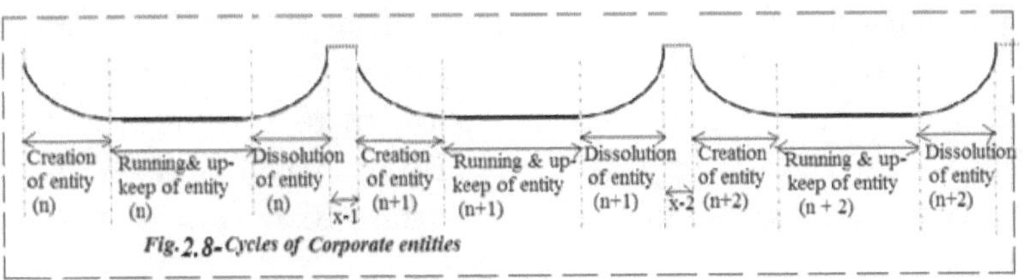

Fig.2.8- Cycles of Corporate entities

~~~~~~~~~~~~~~~~~~~~~~~~~~~~~
~~~~~~~~~~~~~~~~~~~~~~~~~~~~~

3   Overview of Governance

(The faith which is upon us and this is better than us in the world, then it is Hindutva. If we open our hearts and minds for it, then it will be good for us --- By Hudson Smith, year 1919)

As said, Brahma, Vishnu and Shiva are the three forms of Brahman, the Trimurti (or Trideva), the supreme power of universe. The three are, sometimes, also referred as Hiranyagarbha, Isvara and Viraj respectively. They are the three personifications of the facets of the Absolute— i.e. Brahma = Space / Existence (sat), Śiva = Consciousness (chit) & Vishnu = Bliss (ānanda). That is why He is known as "Satchitananda". Each of them has their female consort (feminine energy) and collectively, the three are called 'Tridevi". As the three different faces / forms of same supreme power, Brahman, the three are eternal and un-born. Yet for simplicity and for satisfaction of some wishes, scriptures sometime show them as born to some deity— e.g. Brahma appears from Vishnu's naval, Shiva born as manasputra from Brahma, Vishnu born to Rishi Kardama as Kapila etc.

The roles played by the these three have a similar application in the context of organizational development and organizational life cycle. It is also relevant to corporate culture and change management. The roles of Brahma creating the universe, Vishnu maintaining / preserving and Shiva in dissolving the universe is similar to the roles of leaders in forming an effective organization culture, maintaining and sustaining the culture and changing the culture to adapt to the changing environment and, lastly, organizational renewal / reengineering or disposal. Corporate culture is the total sum of the values, customs, traditions and meanings that make an organization unique. Life in this world is a manifestation of these three principles of creation, preservation and dissolution. The apparent destruction / dissolution is only an essential forerunner to creation. The creation and dissolution are so inseparable that they can be considered as the two sides of same coin, with preservation being the integral part of both.

In today's complex and robot-like and scandal and fraud prone organizational culture, ethical values are now considered among the most important ones to restore the vital trust among their stakeholders, particularly customers and the communities and, as such, strict ethical standards and ethical values need to be prioritized. It starts with selecting carefully and hiring more ethical people, starting from top / leader and creatively identifying specific types of cultural elements, such as symbols, stories and rituals that communicate and reinforce the company's culture. The governance of universe by Hindu Trinity (Brahma, Vishnu, & Shiva) and their associates gives a handy guideline for corporates.

There are several ways to look at the corporate culture vis-à-vis culture of universe, a few of those are given herewith---

1- Historical- Culture is social heritage or tradition that is passed on to future generations. It is critical that the corporate leaders work proactively, up-keeping parts of the past and respecting the past yet relevantly adapt to the present, with some view of future.

2- Behavioral- Culture is shared, is learned human behaviors and becomes a way of life. Focus on the core elements (ethical values) that should not change much overtime.

3- Functional- Culture is the way people solve problems of adapting to the environment, situations and living together.

4- Structural- Culture consists of patterned and interrelated ideas, symbols or behaviors and assigning meanings that are shared by any corporation or even universe.

3.1   Corporate Governance of the Universe

Fig. 3.1 shows separately the positional and functional classification of the Trinity / Trimurti or Brahman. Personal classification is the apparent designations of the three as Creator (Lord Brahma), Preserver (Lord Vishnu) and Destroyer / Annihilator / Dissolution / Guru (Lord Shiva). Considering the 'Yoni-Linga' concept or 'Yin-Yang' concept of Sec.1.3.1 of Masculine and Feminine energies, the functional classification of the Trinity has been shown as their consorts.

Combining the positional with their functional classifications, the three become the complete potent identities to perform their functions effectively.

In Fig.3.1, Lord Brahma as creator and Goddess Saraswathi as knowledge, idea and learning, have been shown in one box. This is because they complement and supplement each other. They are separate but inseparable, as masculine and feminine energy concept of chapter-1. Brahma and Saraswathi, together, signify many things, e.g.-

1- Brahma is the creative will, and Saraswathi is the intelligence (buddhi) that executes the will of Brahma. Together they form the human consciousness and give discretionary and decision-making abilities.

2- Brahma is the Vedas symbolized and Saraswathi is the vibration hidden in the mantras as the sound. Together they constitute the spiritual knowledge of the Vedas.

3- Brahma is the primeval silence of soul, and Saraswathi is the noise/sound of life. Together they create the mortal beings.

4- Brahma creates life while Saraswathi gives social
   structure and refines the individuals with civility and
   grace.

5- Saraswathi is the pearl of wisdom (sara) born in the shell
   of Brahma from a raindrop (swathi). Thus, the name
   Saraswathi has been derived.

We would discuss further about creation aspect in chapter-4.

The maintenance and preservation of the universe requires
plenty of wealth and resources, and as such, the consort of Lord
Vishnu is Lakshmi, who is the goddess of wealth and resources
in abundance. Lakshmi is also considered the Goddess of good
fortune. As the Mother of all abundance, she also manifests
variously and takes many forms, as part of Vishnu's duties as
preserver and sometimes on her own. Together with Lakshmi,
Lord Vishnu becomes all resourceful and capable to preserve the
universe. We will discuss preservation further in chapter-5.

Lord Shiva, the destroyer (rejuvenator) is married to the
Goddess Sakthi. Sakthi represents perishable matter (prakriti).
Lord Shiva's marriage with Goddess Sakthi gives the power of
dissolution / destruction and signifies that the power of
destruction / dissolution has no meaning without its association
with perishable matter. Destruction manifests itself only when
there is perishable matter. Again, the power (Shakti) goes along
with devotion so that the two remain as one. Shakti is also
considered as Isvari, or the Divine Mother. She also takes many
forms, some pleasant and some very fierce and destructive, thus
helping Shiva in dissolution. Lord Shiva's posture symbolizes
perfect inner harmony and poise, experienced by a person of
realization. We would discuss this further in chapter-6.

View- a of Fig.3.1 shows the positional and functional
classification of the three lords and (view- b) shows the same in
the form of bath-tub curve. Of-course, unlike shown in (view- a)
of Fig.3.1, the duration of preservation is much more that the
other two.

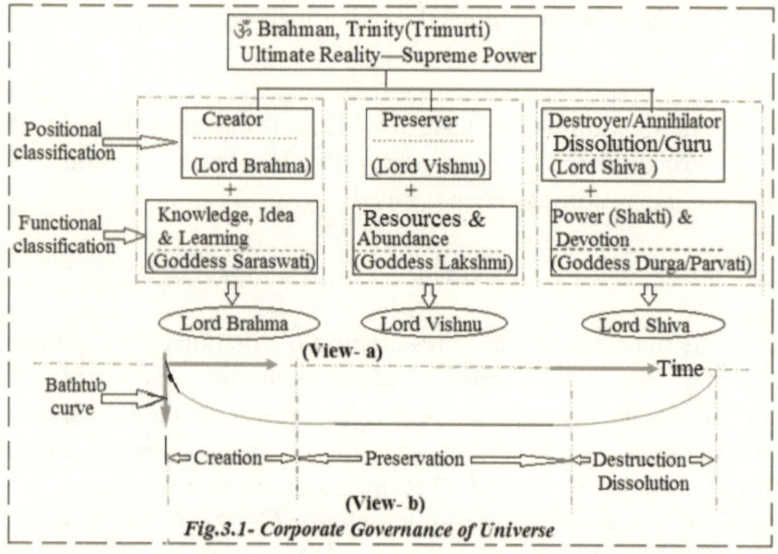

Fig.3.1- Corporate Governance of Universe

3.2   Corporate Governance of a Corporation

Fig.3.2 shows the overview of corporate governance of any corporation or corporate entity. The similarity of governance of universe and governance of corporation, i.e. between Fig. 3.1 and Fig.3.2 is strikingly clear. Like Lord Brahma, I/c Planning & Project should have knowledge, idea and information about the product, process, place, environment and expected constraints. Like Lord Vishnu, I/c Works / Plant should have leadership, skills, established processes, resources (men, material, money and time etc.) and necessary machines and equipment. Like Lord Shiva, I/c General Administration should have authority / power of security, punishment, teaching and development, disposal, liquidation and legal etc. We would discuss some more of these in subsequent chapters.

Here again, Fig.3.2 shows two views. (View a) shows the positional classification, i.e. the rough designation combined with functional classification, i.e. necessary prerequisites / resources for their job and together they make their complete identity in corporation. (View b) shows the same in bathtub curve form.

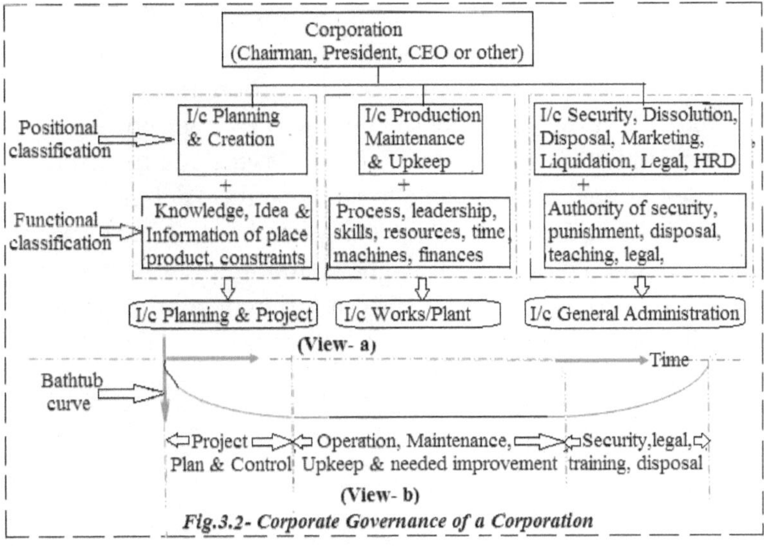

Fig.3.2- Corporate Governance of a Corporation

3.3   Corporate Governance of a Country

The logic of corporate governance of the universe can be extended to running of a country also. Whether a country is newly formed by amalgamation of few small states / colonies or a country is liberated from some colonial rule or any existing country, the method of governance for all can be classified in three categories--- legislative, executive and judiciary. These three broad functions are somewhat similar to corporate governance of the universe, i.e. creation, preservation and dissolution. This has been shown in Fig.3.3. It shows the comparison between the governance of universe and country and the bathtub curve for that.

Legislation is the first step of governance of any country. Legislative functions include making (enact, amend, repeal) basic laws, rules and regulations, examine and approve budget for running the government (execution), approve taxation and public expenditure etc. Once the legislation is done or created, the country is ready for smooth running. It is similar as to once

the universe is created by Lord Brahma, it is ready for
preservation. In most countries, the legislative branch is called
'Parliament'. It is also called 'Congress' (in USA), 'House of
People', 'National Assembly' and so on.

Executive governance is the second function of total
governance. It is responsible for carrying out or administering
laws enacted by the legislature. Its functions include to ensure
domestic tranquility, to provide for the common defense
(internal & external), to promote the general welfare, to establish
justice, foreign diplomacy, etc. to help smooth preservation of a
country. The executive governance of different countries may
differ slightly, but essence remains the same. It is, again, like
'preservation' in the corporate governance of the universe, by
Lord Vishnu.

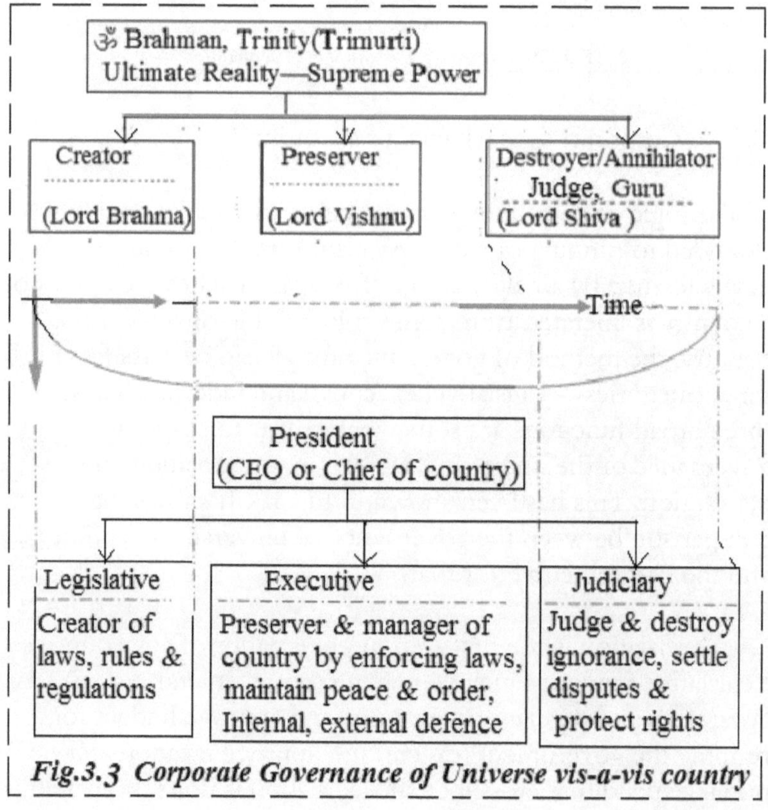

Fig.3.3 Corporate Governance of Universe vis-a-vis country

The main function of judiciary is to interpret the laws as per the constitution and the laws passed by legislation, settle disputes, protect civil and fundamental rights of citizens, and limit the powers of the other branches of government. It has power to award punishment for different types of offences. Its functions may be considered as similar to those of Lord Shiva, who destroys the ignorance for salvation.

In the three-branch system of governance of a country, each has the ability to check the others from getting too powerful and thus help the country to work in balanced way as one entity. This is just similar to Brahma, Vishnu and Shiva working in unison and balanced way as one entity as Trimurti of the universe.

3.4   Corporate Governance of ॐ (Aum or Om)

The character ॐ is pronounced in English as 'Om' or 'Aum'. Om is basically a monosyllabic word, as compared to Aum, which is tri-syllabic. In Sanskrit, 'O' is a diphthong sound. It appears to be formed by combining the two sounds 'A' and 'U'. As such, 'Om' is actually 'Aum', which became 'Om' only due to transliteration.

We do not find any specific mention of Om in early Vedic period, probably because of utmost 'sanctity and purity' attached to it and it was not allowed to be used outside the text of the Vedic sacrifices, but, around the later Vedic period (Yajur Veda), it became customary to use it before any Vedic hymn etc. Though not clearly mentioned, it is said that with their research in 2010 and 2013, NASA recorded some sound, similar to Aum / Om, coming from Sun's atmosphere. That NASA report leads us to assume that some sound like Aum / Om is all the time occurring in the universe (Brahmanda), supposedly coming from that supreme power, i.e. Ultimate Reality.

Aum /Om is the central pillar of Hinduism and the part of its traditions and literature over the ages. It is the essence of all mantras and Vedas and has the sound of infinite Brahman. Aum /Om is the sound of Sun, the sound of Light and the sound of assent (affirmation). The efficacy of Aum / Om is unbound and limitless. It is 'Anahat Nada' or the 'unstruck sound', which refers to sounds that do not cause any obstruction in the oral cavity while they are pronounced. The Aum of Hinduism also possibly became the sacred word of "Hum" of the Buddhists, Amin of the Muslims and Amen for Christians.

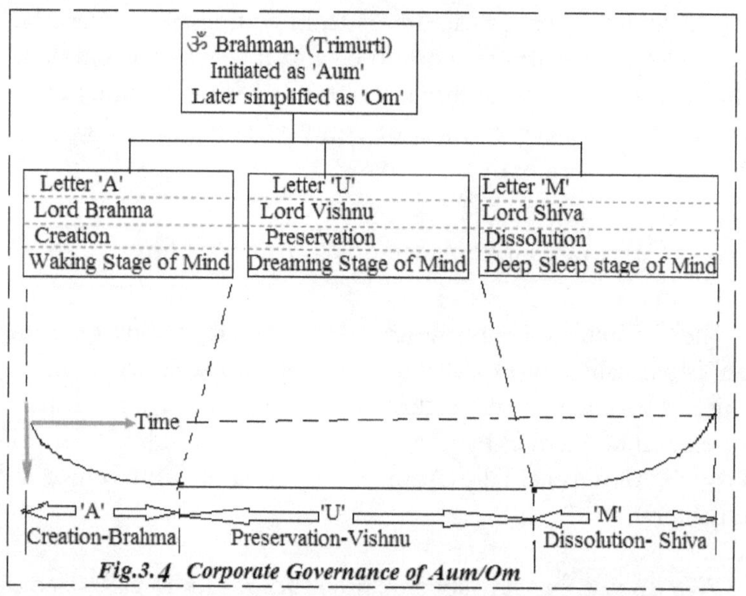

Fig.3.4 Corporate Governance of Aum/Om

Fig.3.4 shows the corporate governance of Aum / Om, which is, again, somewhat similar to corporate governance of the universe and also shows similar bathtub curve. The three stages of creation, preservation and dissolution also refer to 'Waking stage', 'Dreaming stage' and 'Deep sleeping' stage of mind. Also refer Sec.2.1.3.

In mythology, 'Aum' represents the God in totality. It is a part of divinity and represents as such to Trimurti – Brahma, Vishnu and Shiva. 'AUM' is made of three letters / alphabets (which are three stages), A+U+M. Also, while saying 'Aum' properly, it appears that the sound has three parts--- A (as 'aa'), 'U' (as 'ooo') and 'M' (as 'mmm'). The three letters represent creation, preservation and dissolution, same way as Brahma, Vishnu and Shiva. Let us consider the three individually.

1- Sound 'A' (as 'aa')- It is the beginning of all sounds. It is the most common letter that starts alphabets and this sound represents the creation aspect of the universe and all of the objects within it. With this sound, we experience the existence of the world through the activity of the normal senses. As such, this sound is represented by Lord Brahma, the creator of the universe. Again, as the Base Chakra and Sex Chakra are connected with creation aspects of our body, the sound 'aa' appears to be coming out from area around these two chakras. Sound 'A' also represents the 'waking stage' of one's mind.

2- Sound 'U' (as 'ooo')- It signals the maintaining energy and running of the universe and the subtle impressions of the mind. As such, this sound is represented by Lord Vishnu, who is the preserver and maintainer of the universe. Again, as the Solar Plexus Chakra and Heart Chakra are connected with maintenance and running aspects of our body, the sound 'ooo' appears to be coming out from area around these two chakras in chest. It represents cosmos hemisphere inhabiting all deities and gandharvas etc. and beyond our mind and thought and is preserved by Vishnu. In other words, it is our 'dreaming state' of mind.

3- Sound 'M', though considered as one sound 'mmm', appears in two little different sound --- starts with 'umm', with lips open, and finishes with 'mmm', with lips closed. Sound 'umm' portrays the transformative energy of the universe and the knowledge, thoughts and beliefs of our existence. As such, the sound 'umm' appears to be coming from area near the throat chakra. As Lord Shiva, in order to save the world, kept the poison in His throat, our knowledge and thoughts may overpower all negativities of our life.

Sound 'mmm' unites us to the awareness of oneness. It is the vibration which is beyond verbal pronunciation. It is also pure consciousness of the 'Self' or the Atman. As such, this sound appears to be coming from or associated with Brow Chakra and Crown Chakra. Again, Lord Shiva is associated with these attributes as He is the conscious keeper, destroyer and dissolution in-charge.

Total sound 'M' (umm + mmm) stands for dissolution and cessation of all worldly thoughts because we are into complete unconsciousness or 'deep sleep' and is creation or attribute of Shiva. Though we are not conscious but still remember in the morning that we went to sleep or other matters. Thus, uttering properly the whole cycle of Aum / Om and concentrating respective chakras at the same time, may help in activation of our all seven chakras.

The three portions of Aum also represent to the three gunas, which are Rajas, Satvik and Tamas respectively. It also indicates three parts of existence, heaven, earth and netherworld. The syllable Om has endless meaning, explanation and glorification.

3.5   Governance of Life Cycle of Human Beings

Corporate governance of a human being (or, for that reason, any living being, including trees and creatures etc.) can also be considered in the same way as life cycle of universe, i.e. creation, preservation and decay / dissolution. Whatever essential amino acids, carbohydrates, essential fatty acids, and twenty-eight vitamins and minerals we take to sustain our life and health, our body constantly changes and goes through different stages. All these stages can be classified in three categories, as shown in Fig.3.5.

1- Childhood- It is the formation and development stage and includes pregnancy, infancy, toddler, kid and teen years and older adolescence years and generally spans up-to first 20 years. We can also call this period as 'physical stage' as our physique, strength, capability and knowledge are developed which are utilized in next stages. This childhood is clearly similar to the 'creation stage' of Lord Brahma, as shown in the bathtub curve (view-b) of Fig.3.5.

2- Adulthood- It is the preservation, utilization and maintenance stage. It includes 'enterprisc stage' (early adulthood, say 20 ~ 35 years), 'contemplation stage' (midlife stage, say 35 ~ 50 years) and 'benevolence stage' (mature adulthood, say 50 ~ 60 years). In enterprise stage we concentrate on making a home, family, circle of friends and making our mark. In contemplation stage, we consider security, support, rules, regulations and reduce our concentration from worldly responsibilities and move more towards deeper meaning of our lives. In benevolence stage, we try to finish our family responsibilities and try to become contributors to the betterment of society through volunteerism, mentorships, and other forms of philanthropy. Because of these, the total adulthood is also known as psychological stage. This, again, is similar to preservation stage (Lord Vishnu) of Fig. 3.5 (view-b)

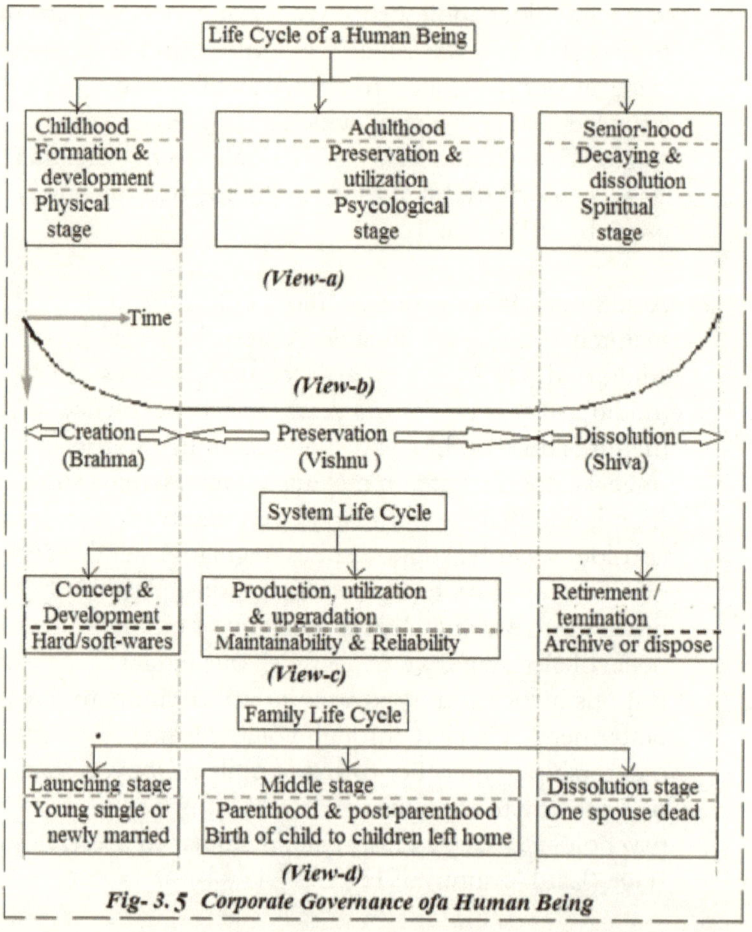

Fig- 3. 5 *Corporate Governance of a Human Being*

3- Senior-hood- It is the decay and dissolution stage (say 60 years till death). It includes mainly 'mature or wisdom stage', because of richness of experience and 'dying stage', because of losing strength, vitality and losing control over our own body. We, sometime, develop boredom and disenchantment of the pleasures of the world and move to containment towards God or supreme power, enlightenment, awakening of true nature. As such, this stage is also called as 'Spiritual stage'. This stage, again, correspond to 'Dissolution stage' of Lord Shiva.

Few create another stage as 'Elderhood' which, actually, include later part of adulthood and early part of senior-hood.

The above-mentioned logic can be extended to most of the activities / situations of human being. Here we have considered two such cases, i.e. 'system life cycle' and 'family life cycle', shown as 'View-c' and 'View-d' of Fig. 3.5.

3.5.1   Governance of System Life Cycle

(View-c of Fig.3.5)

The system life cycle, in systems (or even a product) engineering, is a view of a system that addresses all phases of its existence, including system conception, design and development / construction, production, utilization and operation, maintenance and needed upgradation, distribution, sales, support, retirement, phase-out and disposal. Just like a human being, we may put any amount of intelligence at design / development stage and take any amount of care and improvement while using it, the system (or the product), one day, will be dissolved (phased-out, archive or disposal) for various reasons. Thus, the total life cycle of any system can, again, be grouped in following three categories—

1- Concept & development stage (Creation, i.e. Lord Brahma stage)- This period, though short, includes initiation, conceptualization, Planning, needed analysis, design, development, testing, integration and assessing financial viability.

2- Production & utilization stage (Preservation, i.e. Lord Vishnu stage)- This period, supposedly long, include implementation, production / operation, maintenance, inspection, needed upgradation/repairs, distribution, sales, support, safety, environment and legal aspects and on-going financial monitoring etc.

3- Retirement / Termination stage (Dissolution, i.e. Lord Shiva stage)- This stage is reached when the system (or product) becomes uneconomical or unsafe or obsolete / unworthy or unrepairable or un-relevant or new better and cheaper alternatives come-up. This period includes phasing-out and keeping in storage / archive or destroyed & disposed-off.

3.5.2 Governance of Family Life Cycle

(View-d of Fig.3.5)

The family life cycle is a series of stages through which a family may pass over time and the emotional and intellectual stages one passes through from childhood to retirement years as a member of a family. It includes the periods of a single young adult, a newly married couple, a family with young children, a family with adolescents, bringing-up the children, divorce & remarriage (if any), and the later declining stage of till dissolution, i.e. death of one or both spouses. The total life cycle can again be grouped in following three similar categories—

1- Launching stage (similar as Creation, i.e. Lord Brahma stage)- It is the creation of family. This period includes young singles, dating & newly married couples. This is also called 'bachelor' stage and may extend up-to 30 years or more.

2- Middle stage (similar as Preservation, i.e. Lord Vishnu stage)- It is like preservation of family and may extend up-to 65 years of age. This stage carries on the basic functions of a family, i.e. sexual needs, home, procreation and rearing of children, economic needs, socialization and security, cultural & religious, helping children to settle and, often, leave parent's home etc. Early period of this stage is parenthood and later as post-parenthood, i.e. full-nest and empty-nest. This is true for both couples and single parents.

3- Dissolution stage (similar as Dissolution, i.e. Lord Shiva stage)- After the empty-nest (all children left home) and because of physiological decline, the concept of family starts losing significance. Retirement from active job also creates a feeling that our role is coming to an end and disposition of some of the assets start. This stage, often, has to deal with loss of siblings and peers. Ultimately the family dissolves with the death of one or both spouses.

~~~~~~~~~~~~~~~~~~~~~~~
~~~~~~~~~~~~~~~~~~~~~~~

4   Creation aspects of Universe and Corporation

(The entire world will accept Hindu religion one day and if it cannot even accept the real name it will accept it by name only--- Bernard Shaw, 1856 - 1950)

For creation purpose, universe can broadly be classified in two groups— 'hardware' and 'software' or 'living and associated things' and 'non-living and associated things', as mentioned in Table T-2.1. For modern science, creation of hardware portion may not be that difficult to explain, but the creation of software portion is rather difficult to explain. For our discussions, we would, mostly, consider universe in totality, including both, hardware and software and occasionally the software alone, i.e. life aspect of universe.

For discussion of creation aspects of universe or any corporate entity (industry, facility, establishment and organization etc.) six basic questions are considered--- 'What', 'Who', 'Why', 'How', When' and 'Where'. We have already discussed 'What is Universe' and 'What is corporation' in chapter-2. In this chapter we will discuss mainly the questions 'Who', 'Why' and 'How'. The remaining two questions, 'Where' and 'When' will, roughly, be built in our previous three questions.

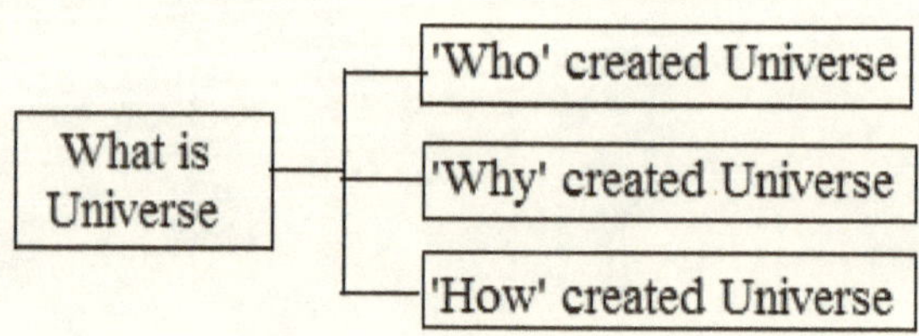

4.1   Who created the Universe (Scientific Lens)

Some people (past and present) argue that it is irrelevant and fruitless to discuss about who created the universe--- the universe existed as it is all along and will continue to exist as it is. Since ages and generations, the Sun has been rising in the morning and setting in evening, moon changing from full moon to no-moon and again to full moon, the people / animals taking birth and dying after some time, the trees sprouting from seed, blossoming and the dying and fresh tree coming out from their seeds, seasons come and go --- all in almost similar cyclic pattern. Even the so-called calamities, like storm and cyclone etc. also occur in somewhat similar pattern since ages. They don't see any reason to believe that the Universe was different earlier. As such, they say that the universe has been existing all along and is eternal, so where is the question of who created universe. Similar 'no creator' concept is advocated by few intelligent scientists and philosophers, like Aristotle, who don't believe (or don't want to believe) the existence of all mighty God and say that the universe had existed forever and something eternal is more perfect than something created. However, explaining the origin of the universe is an enormous challenge for those seeking to deny its Creator.

But many scientists and philosophers ultimately believe that there is some intelligent supreme power who created the universe and keep it going. Three type of theories are put in favor of this---

1- Earlier people thought that the universe is static and not expanding. But around 1929, Edwin Hubble published a law relating the rate of recession of different galaxies and their distance from us and concluded that the universe is expanding. This was not caused by some accidental force thrusting them away from each other. Rather, they are still moving. Later, few other scientists agreed that though the galaxies are bound by gravitational forces and the galaxies within itself would keep their size and configuration, the distance and space between various galaxies is continuously expanding and different galaxies are moving away from each other. If that is true, then the universe must have been smaller in the past. In fact, if we extrapolate to the distant past, all the matter and energy in the universe would have been concentrated in a very tiny region of unimaginable density and temperature, i.e. the universe moving backward into the past, getting tinier and tinier until it come upon a creation event, a time when it all began—the event we now call the big bang. Creation of such a big universe from nothing or from nowhere and then maintaining regularities in the motion of so many astronomical bodies, is impossible without some intelligent supreme power / authority involved in that. We may call that creator of universe as God or Brahman, prime mover of universe or anything as mentioned chapter-1.

2- The Laws of Thermodynamics, the most fundamental laws of the physical sciences, gives a good evidence that the universe had a beginning. The two laws are---

- 1st Law: The total amount of mass-energy in the universe is constant.
- 2nd Law: The amount of energy available for work is running out, or *entropy* is increasing to a maximum.

If the total amount of mass-energy is limited, and the amount of usable energy is decreasing, then the universe cannot have existed forever, otherwise it would already have exhausted all usable energy—the 'heat death' of the universe. For example, all radioactive atoms would have decayed, every part of the universe would be the same temperature, and no further work would be possible. So, the obvious corollary is that the universe began a finite time ago with huge/unimaginable amount of usable energy from nothing, which can only be possible for some super-natural supreme power, we may call God or anything.

3- It is said that about 200-300 million years after the creation of the universe (say Big Bang), the only one star exploded in a supernova. Then other stars were created, and the first galaxy formed at about 1 billion years after the Big Bang. Then other galaxies were created. Our Solar System was not created until 9 billion years later and earth is estimated to be about 4.5 billion years old. Combining various theories, a logical conclusion would state clearly that all forces, matter and beyond came from one single source. The source is an intelligent superbeing who makes decisions and is very patient. This superbeing has at His disposal an infinite amount of energy. Without His intervention, no stage in the development of the early universe would have been possible. For example, the central original mass would have remained the same and never expanded giving us the Big Bang. The clouds of gas and smoke would have remained the same and no stars or galaxies would have formed. The so called 'Dark Matter' and 'Dark Energy' (refer Sec.2.1.1), which is over 90% of mass of universe and which have never been seen or measured by any scientist, are nothing but the energy and capabilities of our that superbeing, the creator of the universe. We may call him God or Brahman or anything.

Many physicists and cosmologists have started accepting that the whole cosmos is a single continuous entity, working in a logical harmony like the human body. The individual cells of each part of our body (say brain, heart, liver etc.) are linked to the entire body and if we look one cell in isolation, its relationship with whole body is lost. Each part does two things simultaneously—at local level, they keep the individual cell alive and at holistic level, they keep the entire body alive. Similarly, the individual constituents of entire cosmos work in two ways—one, at local level, maintaining its own domain and at holistic level, help in keeping the entire cosmos working as one body. As an example, the Sun, at local level, controls its own domain (Solar System) and, at holistic level, plays its part in our galaxy and in turn, the entire universe. Again, just like humans can't exist without birth and death, creation and destruction, the stars and galaxies also undergo birth and death—their life cycle is only a matter of shuffling matter and energy around in the cosmic universe. As such, for easy understanding of our lesser educated people, the ancient saints in India personified the whole cosmos, including multi-universe, as the body of one supreme power, say "Maha-Vishnu" and the individual constituents of universe emerging and working as different parts of body of Maha-Vishnu.

4.2   Who created the Universe (Mythological Lens)

With reference to the previous section, answering this question, from mythological angle, is rather easy. Hinduism and most religions / cultures speak of some supreme power or ultimate reality, having infinite energy and resources, created the universe and everything in it, from Himself. We may call him God, Brahman, Paramatman, Maha-Vishnu, Sada-Siva, Maha-Shakti, Purusha, Allah or anything. He, being of infinite resources, remains infinite even after all creation from himself. It is our nature that when, in-spite of our all efforts, we can't find the cause of some happening, we leave it to God, or say that God has done it. Some Hindu scriptures convey the indefinable nature of this creator by saying "That One Thing, breathless, breathed by its own nature".

4.3   Who creates the Corporation

Theoretically, any individual can start a corporation and he would be called a promotor. But a big corporation is a wholly separate legal entity. This means that the business is actually viewed as being separate and distinct from the individuals who run the corporation (the board of directors etc.). While the board runs the corporation, shareholders own the corporation, but that does not give them the right to be involved in the day-to-day management of the company. For Government or Semi-government corporate entities, the shares are normally owned by the President of the country and in turn the shares, theoretically, are owned by individual citizens of the country. The Board of

Directors appoint the Chairman or CEO (Chief Executive Officer) of the corporate entity and he/she starts the creation process of that entity. The Chairman or CEO, with approval of Board, appoints I/c Planning & Creation, who takes up further creation jobs.

This is somewhat similar to creator of Universe, where the Board of Directors, Chairman and CEO were all in one, i.e. Brahman, the Supreme Power, the Ultimate Reality and creator of the universe was designated by Him as Brahma.

4.4   Why Universe was created

From scientific angle, it has not been clearly established why universe has been created. Those group of modern science, who believe that universe is not a created item, i.e. it existed forever, and it will exist forever, there is no question as to 'why universe has been created'. For some other group of modern science, who doesn't believe in any creator of universe, but agree that universe has a 'beginning', i.e. it has been created or come to an existence by some accident or chance (say Big Bang etc.), the question of 'why somebody has caused that accident or chance' doesn't arise. But it is self-evident that things that begin have a cause— no-one really denies it in his heart. All science and history would collapse if this 'law of cause and effect' (also referred as Law of Karma) were denied. Also, the universe cannot be self-caused— nothing can create itself, because that would mean that it existed before it came into existence, which is, rather, absurd. A Universe without any reason or purpose would have no stability or trustworthiness. As such, this group of people has yet to find out why such accident or chance took place without believing that there was (and is) a super-controller or creator.

Many people of modern science, ultimately, agree that some 'Supreme Power' termed as 'God' has created or caused creation of universe. They say that God, unlike the universe, had no beginning, so doesn't need a cause. Since God is the creator of time also, He is not limited by the time dimension. Of-course, once the universe has been created, the time and universe depend on each other, i.e. we can't have time without universe and, also, we can't have universe without time. As God is beyond time dimension, He need-not or doesn't have a cause. True, but the Universe is a created one, so it should have a cause. No creator creates anything without any reason or purpose. However, they are still not clear about the motive of creation.

We have almost agreed in previous section that 'God' is the creator. Then the immediate answer as to 'why God created Universe' is that creation is the basic attribute of creator. A creator who does not create is something of a contradiction in terms. This is not to say that God needs His creation. God is free from all needs. It is the creation which needs God. Mankind doesn't really create; they merely manipulate what already exists – what was already created by God. Only God alone creates from nothing. Even the artist 'creates' designs based on what he has seen in some form or other. It is not possible to imagine what has not been perceived by the senses. Even in dream, we, mostly, see only those things / persons which we have seen, heard, experienced / felt or thought in some form or other and hardly see something absolutely new and unconnected. God created both, angels (normally incapable to committing sins) and mankind (capable to making mistakes) and wish that when mankind make sin / mistake, they should take refuge in Him (God) and beg for God's divine attribute of mercy, forgiveness and love.

It is easier to answer this question from mythological angle. Bible and some other scriptures say that God created the Universe for His glory and pleasure and He desired to share His life with others. All things were created by Him and for Him. So, He created Human being (and also other living creatures), in both masculine and feminine forms / energies, as image of God or reflector of God and wanted the World (Universe) to be filled up by His reflectors. God created the World (Universe) in perfect balance and wanted His reflectors to choose to perform godly acts, thereby becoming godlier and acquiring merits; but somehow it went wrong so God sent His messenger (prophet) to the World to do quick rescue job and show His glory. However, it should be remembered that being created for God's pleasure does not mean humanity was made to entertain God or provide Him with amusement. Truly He is free from all need, pleasure or pain. God is a creative Being, and it gives Him pleasure to create and be in genuine relationship with what He created.

Vedic and Hinduism scriptures also say that God made the Universe for His entertainment and enjoyment. But His entertainment is not like human's, i.e. to kill time. God is beyond time and need not kill it. The enjoyment of pure love is the climax of all entertainments and this climax is called as a specific bliss. Hence, the sole purpose of God creating Universe was to enjoy this specific bliss. God already has this variety of bliss. But, when this type of bliss comes in a scene showing devotees proving their real love to God, the bliss is really enjoyable. For such scene, God alone is not sufficient. Something and somebody other than God, i.e. various entities of His creation, various souls and the cosmic energy, also must exist. For experiencing the entertainment and bliss and also to share His happiness, God Himself enters into each human, thus each soul becomes a part of God.

As said in chapter-1, there is one basic difference between Hinduism and Christianity and many others--- God doesn't send any special messenger or Son or prophet in Hinduism. Each and every living soul is a part or messenger of God. Refer to Sec.1.3.2 for different souls- Atman and Jivatma.

4.5   Why Corporation is created

In general, a corporation is created / formed to promote, stimulate, develop and advance the business prosperity and economic welfare of share / stake holders in particular and public in general; to promote the business development and maintain the economic stability of the society, provide maximum opportunities for employment, and improve the standard of living of the people in general.

Apparently, the reason for creating a universe and for creating a corporation looks much different, but going in the spirit and root cause, the two are not much different. God created the universe so that He shares His enjoyment, happiness and bliss with all the humans and others He has created. Similarly, the corporation is created for sharing the profits, entertainments, welfares and opportunities etc. with all the stakeholders and other concerned public.

As mentioned earlier, corporations are of different types— public companies, private companies, government business enterprises, municipal corporations, charities and foundations etc. As such, purpose of their creation may be somewhat different. In general followings are be the reasons for creating a corporation-

1- Limited liability for stakeholders/owners
2- Income / facility / welfare splitting and sharing
3- Central Management, Corporate Structure and better control
4- Flexibility and transferability of ownership
5- Asset Protection and upkeep
6- Perpetual / long-lasting duration of the entity
7- Credibility and prestige.

4.6 How Universe was created (Scientific Lens)

We would discuss in following four sub-sections—

4.6.1 Timeline for Evolution of Universe and Mankind

Fig.4.1 shows in brief as to how the universe and Mankind evolved. Taking the 'Big Bang' theory of creation, the Universe was created some 13.5 billion years ago. That was the time when any matter (atoms & molecules) was created. As per Hinduism, that was the time when Lord Maha-Vishnu caused imbalance in the three Gunas of Prakriti. Refer Sec. 4.7. The Universe continued expanding and our planet, 'Earth' was formed about 4.5 billion years ago. Because of some chance combination of necessary ingredients / elements, some sort of life (organism) appeared on Earth about 3.5 billion years ago. The life form continued to develop and about 2.5 million years ago, early human form (Homo) evolved and, with them, 'stone age' started. After that, about 2.4 million years ago, 'Ice Age' started. About 3,00,000 years ago, Homo sapiens (anatomically modern humans) emerged, somewhere in Africa. Neanderthals and some other human species also emerged in other part of Earth. Also, daily use of 'fire' was started by those humans. About 70,000 years ago, cognitive uprising occurred, and those humans developed fictional and illustrative languages. Because of their superior brain, better language and communication skill and better group formation, Homo sapiens spread to other parts of Earth and Neanderthals and other human species were eliminated / vanished between the period 45,000 to 13,000 years ago. Our present generation is the descendent of that Homo Sapiens. As they settled in different part of Earth, their color, creed, race and culture etc. varied because of different weather and geographic situations.

About 12,000 years ago, the old stone-age and Ice-age ended and with that the agriculture uprising started. People started living in permanent settlements and animal domestication started. Gradually kingdoms and civilizations started. About 5500 years ago two oldest and well-known civilizations were Mesopotamian and Indus Valley civilizations. That followed the start of Bronze-age, about 5300 years ago. About 3500 years ago, Vedic Era (leading to Hinduism) started. (Some say that Vedic Era / Hinduism started about 7000 years ago, i.e. 5000BCE). Then, about 2800 years ago, Iron-age started. Between the period of 2500 to 1400 years ago, Buddhism, Taoism, Christianity and Islam started. Then the modern Era started, with the start of scientific revolution about 500 years back and Industrial revolution, about 250 years back.

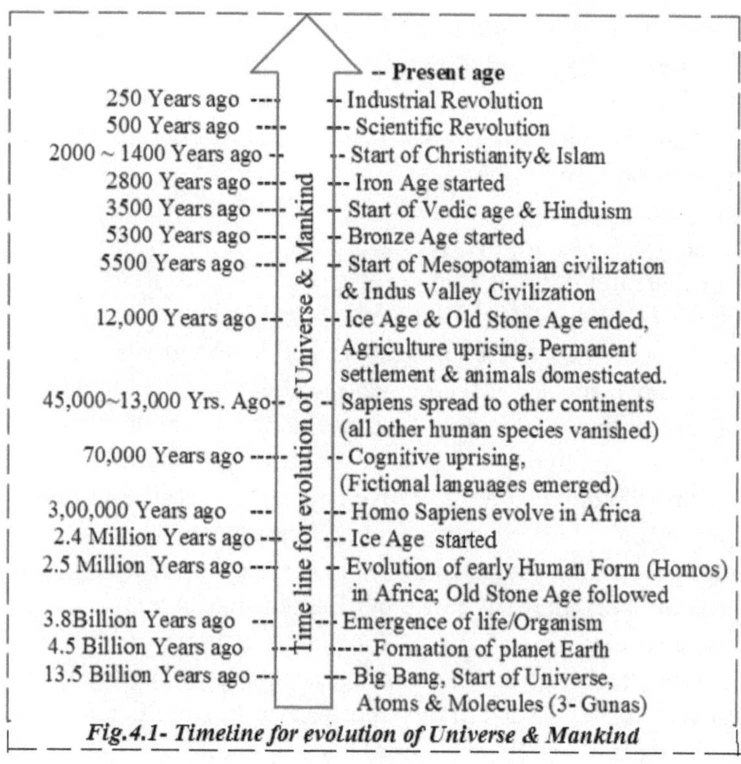

Fig.4.1- Timeline for evolution of Universe & Mankind

4.6.2 Formation / Evolution of Universe

How and when did the universe begin? Probably no other scientific question provokes such spirited debate among researchers. After all, no one was around when the universe began, so who can say what really happened? The best that scientists can do is work out possible theory, backed up by observations of the universe. So far, no one has come up with an undisputable explanation of how the cosmos came to be.

There are quite a few theories on creation of universe and the 'Big Bang Theory' is the most accepted theory, even though quite old. For centuries scientists thought the Universe always existed in a largely unchanged form, but in 1927, George Lemaitre of Belgium said that the Universe began as a large, pregnant and primeval atom, exploding and sending out the smaller atoms that we see today. Before that the so called universe was an extremely hot, small, and dense super-force (the mix of the four fundamental forces- gravity, electromagnetism, weak nuclear force and strong nuclear force). Around 13.8 billion years ago, all the matter in the Universe emerged from a single, minute point (extreme dense super-force with intense gravitational pressure or singularity), in a violent burst (sudden expansion), called Big Bang. This expanded at an astonishingly high rate and temperature, creating space as it rapidly inflated. Within a tiny fraction of a second gravity and all the other forces were formed. Energy changed into particles of matter and antimatter, which largely destroyed each other. But, luckily, some matter survived. Protons and neutrons started to form within the first second; within minutes these protons and neutrons could fuse and form hydrogen and helium nuclei. After many years, nuclei could finally capture electrons to form atoms, filling the Universe with clouds of hydrogen and helium gas. Atoms of elements (calcium, phosphorous, iron, cobalt, nickel etc.) first circulated as interstellar dust and, then, gravity and some other fundamental forces caused them to clump together Again, after many years, it left behind a bath of photons – the Cosmic Microwave Background. Within this bath of photons were tiny ripples of matter that were stretched to enormous sizes during inflation, and in turn these became the seeds for the galaxies and galactic clusters we see today. About 200-300 million years after the creation of the universe, the only star exploded in a supernova. Then other stars were created, and the first galaxy formed at about 1 billion years after the Big Bang. Subsequently, other galaxies were formed. Our Solar System was not created until 9 billion years later and earth is estimated to be about 4.6 billion years old. As already mentioned in Sec.2.1.1, in addition to the "normal" matter that makes up the visible parts of the universe, scientists have discovered that there are vast amounts of unseen and un-understood matters, so-called, "dark matter" (23%) and "dark energy" (72%) and the visible universe account for only about 4.6% ~ 5% of the total. Dark matter makes up about 80% of mass and thus holds the galaxy together and prevent it falling apart.

Again, as already discussed in Sec.4.1, the universe is still expanding continuously, even though the galaxies are bound by gravitational forces and the galaxies within itself would keep their size and configuration.

Though widely accepted, Big Bang Theory also has few inconsistencies / lacunas. Few say that the universe is not that old as given in Big Bang, telling that spiral galaxies should not exist if they are billions of years old. Again, Saturn's rings still look new and shiny, Etc. Again, how can such a big universe come from nothing. As such, scientists tried to explore other theories for creation of universe. Three of such theories are given below----

1- Steady State Theory- It was proposed in 1948 by British scientists Sir Hermann Bondi, Thomas Gold, and Sir Fred Hoyle. It says that the universe is always expanding but maintaining a constant average density, with matter being continuously created to form
new stars and galaxies at the same rate that old ones become unobservable as a consequence of their increasing distance and velocity of recession. A steady-state universe has no beginning or end in time, and from any point within it the view on the grand scale— i.e. the average density and arrangement of galaxies— is the same. Galaxies of all possible ages are intermingled. The advantage of Steady State theory over some other theories is its simple and aesthetic explanations of certain troublesome topics. For example, since the universe is unchanging throughout time, the universe needs no elaborated explanation of its beginning. However, observations since the 1950s (most notably, those of the cosmic microwave background) have produced much evidence contradictory to the steady-state picture and have led scientists to overwhelmingly support the big-bang model.

2- Eternal Inflation theory- After the Big Bang, the universe expanded rapidly during a brief period called inflation.

The Eternal Inflation theory, developed by Alan Guth in 1980, postulates that inflation never stopped and has been going on for an infinite length of time. Somewhere, even now, new universes are coming into existence in a vast complex called the multiverse. Those many universes could have different physical laws. However, this theory can be considered as an extension of Big Bang Theory.

3- Oscillating Universe Theory- Originally conceived by Albert Einstein in 1930, it postulates a universe following an eternal series of oscillations, each beginning with a big bang and ending with a big crunch; in the interim, the universe would expand for a period of time before the gravitational attraction of matter causes it to collapse back in and undergo a bounce. Although this cyclic model differs from the conventional big bang–inflationary model in terms of the physical processes that shape the universe and the whole outlook on cosmic history, both theories match all current observations with the same degree of precision. Probably this theory cannot predict how the universe began, but only how it will evolve once it has begun. We have already discussed similar concept in Sec.2.5.

However, most of the scientific theories for creation of universe try to explain this complex phenomenon by using some assumptions, which may be no better than superstitions. Often such theories are misleading and that is one reason why scientists are often changing or updating their conclusions, calling them new discoveries. Such contradictions lead us to fall back on mythological reasons.

4.6.3   What existed (or came) before the Big Bang

On this question, few scientists opined that it was not necessarily 'pure nothingness' or emptiness. Quantum theory and its derivatives state that the vacuum is not emptiness at all. It is filled with quantum 'stuff'. The quantum vacuum is as filled with quantum stuff containing vast amount of energy not manifesting in observable universe. The big bang might have been caused by such 'stuff' of quantum vacuum, having unimaginable energy. Again, few modern scientists/philosophers opine that before Big Bang, a pre-created state of consciousness exited, which had no dimensions. In this state, consciousness was pure potential and every possibility existed in seed form. It is this potential in consciousness that grew from seed form into every variety of living being. Vedic/Hindu mythology terms that pure consciousness as Supreme Power (say Maha Vishnu). Refer also to Sec. 2.1.4.

4.6.4   Emergence / Evolution of Life on Earth

'How did humankind come to inhabit this Earth' has always been a puzzling question. Were we put here by a Creator? Did we evolve from simpler forms of life? Could we have migrated here from another planet? Francis Crick advocated a theory of "directed panspermia" in 1973--the possibility that an older civilization sent a mission to start life on our newly evolving planet and suggested that we may have cousins on planets which are not too distant. Here we would discuss mainly from scientific lens. From mythological lens, we would discuss later in this chapter.

In today's scientific world, we seem to be on the verge of completely losing our sense of divine origin and purpose as more and more people accept the verdict of "Darwin's Theory of Evolution", even though it quite old (1859) and has lot of contradictions,---that we are the chance result of billions of years of evolution from single-celled creatures, to sea-born creatures, to reptiles, birds, mammals, to apes and finally to human. Charles Darwin brought forward ancient Greek philosophers (such as Anaximander's) theory which postulated the development of life from non-life and the evolutionary descent of man from animal. Darwin's theory tells that all life is related and has descended from a common ancestor: the birds and the bananas, the fishes and the flowers — all related. Darwin's theory presumes the development of life from non-life and stresses a purely naturalistic (undirected and purely chance happening) "descent with modification". That is, complex creatures evolve from more simplistic ancestors naturally over time. In a nutshell, as random genetic mutations occur within an organism's genetic code, the beneficial mutations are preserved because they aid survival — a process known as "natural selection". Natural selection acts only by taking advantage of slow and slight successive variations; it can never take a big and sudden leap. These beneficial mutations are passed on to the next generation. Over time, beneficial mutations accrue, and the result is an entirely different organism (not just a variation of the original, but an entirely different creature). Natural selection is the preservation of a functional advantage that enables a species to compete better in the wild. Natural selection is the naturalistic equivalent to domestic breeding, in which human breeders have produced dramatic changes in domestic animal populations by selecting individuals to breed. Similar things happen in vegetation. In all these, the undesirable traits and inferior species gradually get eliminated and only the superior ones survive.

As some criticism arose and no fossil records and evidence found for the intermediate connecting links between different species, scientists revised Darwin's theory with their "Punctuated Equilibrium" evolutionary theory, supposedly making evolution invisible in the fossil record. Yet this theory is not verifiable in any way and is highly speculative and, in a way, based on unscientific foundations.

There have been quite a few other theories for evolution of life on Earth, though not so detailed and not well taken. One such theory is briefly mentioned below-

* 'Chemical evolution of life' theory by Alexander Oparin from Russia and JBS Haldane from England- It said that the generation of life on earth was a slow chemical process which occurred from pre-existing non-living materials such as amino acids, proteins and nuclear material such as RNA. They suggested that these organic materials came together under conditions of high temperature, reducing atmosphere (without oxygen) and gases released from

volcanos all of which were favorable to produce simple living forms. So, this mixture of organic materials was called as 'organic soup'.

The Miller-Urey Experiment, conducted by Stanley Miller and Harold Urey, in 1952, supported Oparin's and Haldane's hypothesis that putative conditions on the primitive Earth favored chemical reactions that synthesized more complex organic compounds from simpler inorganic precursors. However, there are not many takers of this theory.

4.7   How Universe was created (Hindu Mythology Lens)

This has been discussed briefly in Sec.2.1.3. In Vedic / Hindu mythology all lives come from top—the God or the Supreme Power, Supreme Consciousness. The expansion or development of universe originates from His spiritual elements. He, with these spiritual elements, exist prior to, during and after the material creation. The spiritual plane is eternal, but the material plane is temporary and is submissive to and permeated by the unlimited spiritual energy. The energies of matter and spirit are energies that vibrate at different frequencies and manifest on different levels. Though the scientific approach says that creation of universe is a "process of evolution", Vedic / Hindu approach can be said as "process of inverse evolution".

Though Hinduism, in general, believe that God, the 'Supreme Power' created the Universe, it has somewhat varying viewpoints about creation, origin of life and evolution, mainly due to the dynamic diversity of Hinduism, derived from amalgamation of Vedic people with natives and migrant Aryans. Even different scriptures of Hinduism differ on creation aspect. The early Hindu theories of creation of universe (world) coincided, more or less, with the evolution of religious thought in Vedic India. In the early Vedic hymns, we see descriptions of Aditi as the universal mother or mother goddess. She gave birth to all the gods who in turn shaped or carved the world. The gods were like carpenters or blacksmiths, having super-skills in all trades, who forged and carved the worlds and their beings. This theory developed because they were preoccupied more with the problems of survival rather than with such philosophical speculation as to how the gods and the world came into existence. In the later Vedic hymns, we find a shift from the concrete to the abstract and find descriptions of an absolute self or an infinite being as the efficient and material cause of all creation.

Because of dynamic diversity of Hinduism, we find little difference in followers of 'Advaita' and 'Dvaita' (refer Sec.1.3.2) and also followers of Maha-Vishnu (Vaishnavism), Sada-Shiva (Saivism) and Maha-Shakti (Shaktism) about 'how the universe was created'. However, we consider all the three as different names / forms of the same supreme power, Brahman and we would try to project somewhat common explanation of creation. Again, in chapter-2, we have discussed concept of 'cycle of universe' and 'multi-universe' (many universes existing at the same time). In case of multi-universe also, the creator is the same supreme power, say Maha-Vishnu. For our further discussion, we would consider only one universe, say n^{th} universe of chapter 2.

The creation of universe has been mentioned briefly in Sec.2.5 of chapter-2. Before the creation of universe, there was nothing but the creator, say Maha-Vishnu or Purusha, lying / existing in peace and equilibrium. Prakriti (the prime material energy of which all matter is composed, also called as nature), which is a part of Maha-Vishnu (Purusha) also lying in peace with respect to all the three gunas (tributes / qualities) of any being, i.e. Sattvic (purity, goodness), Rajasic (passion, action, dimness) and Tamasic (darkness, destruction) in perfect balance and equilibrium. All previous existence lay dissolved in Maha-Vishnu as a result of previous Mahapralaya. It has been said in chapter-1 that all the souls (Atman) are part of same Maha-Vishnu, and as such, they never die, but ultimately merge in Maha-Vishnu. When the universe is created again, they take different shape as per their earlier Karma. "Maya", which is one of the tattvas of Prakriti, clouds their true consciousness and makes them behave like limited beings, separate from Maha-Vishnu. Maya (illusion) is a fundamental concept in Hindu philosophy and it means the powerful force that creates the cosmic illusion that the phenomenal world is real. Maya keep us in illusion as to what is our true identity. This sort of forgetting is one of the main principles of the material world, without which the living beings could not engage in material life.

Prakriti is described as unmanifest, primordial matter, which is subtler than the gross realm of quantum physics. As already discussed in chapter-1, Purusha and Prakriti are the masculine and feminine energies of the same supreme power, say Maha-Vishnu.

Some physicists now agree that the three gunas (Triguna) relates to sub-atomic particles of 'atom', i.e. electrons, neutrons, protons. Those three are of the same three qualities: one is of the quality of light – sattva, stability; another is of the quality of rajas - activity, energy, force; and the third is of the quality of inertia and entropy - tamas. The whole world consists of these three gunas; and through these three gunas, a man's awareness has to pass.

4.7.1   Evolution of Universe thru Prakriti

When, due to wish of Maha-Vishnu or otherwise, a disturbance/imbalance in the three gunas occurs, resulting in the formation of subtle imperceptible matter, called the 'Maha-Tattva'. We can also say that this happens over a period of time through the differentiation and combination of the Mahabhutas, Janandriyas, karmendriyas, tanmantras, manas (mind), ahamkara (deluded self) and buddhi (discriminating intelligence). The subtle matter, though can't be perceived by our normal senses, forms the basis of all creation. This 'Maha-Tattva' (also called consciousness), along with intelligence (Buddhi) and the sense of 'Ego' (Ahamkra), is the germinating place of all creation. Lord Brahma is said to be formed from this 'Maha Tattva' and come out from naval of Maha-Vishnu. This disturbance/ imbalance in three gunas of Maha-Vishnu can be compared to "Big Bang" of scientific theory. Brahma, then starts creating the whole universe, by taking the ingredients and energy from infinite resources and energy of Maha-Vishnu.

As per Bhagvad Purana, multiple universes emerge from the infinite pores of the cosmic body of Maha-Vishnu, when He exhales. He, again, enters in each of the egg-shaped universe and in each universe, He is termed as 'Garbhodak-shayi Vishnu'. The universe keeps expanding and maintaining itself as long as Maha-Vishnu continues to exhale. When Maha-Vishnu starts inhaling, the universe starts contracting and finally gets destroyed and dissolved into His cosmic body. This exhalation and inhalation of Maha-Vishnu validates the scientific theory of "expansion and contraction of universe". The period of one exhalation and inhalation of Maha-Vishnu is same as one Brahma-Day, mentioned in Sec.2.5.

Fig.4.2 shows that from Maha-Tattva (or Mahat-Tattva) three types of Ahamkara (Ego) are generated- Vaikarika (Pure from Sattvic Guna), Taijasa (Passionate, from combination of Sattva and Rajasic Gunas) and Butandi (Rudimental, from Tamasic Guna). Vaikarika gives rise to 'Mana' (Mind), Taijasa give rise to 5- Jnanendriya (Cognitive senses) and 5- Karmendriya (Organs of action) and Butandi gives rise to 5- Tanmatras (Subtle elements). The Butandi, in association with each Tanmatra, give rise to 5- Bhutas (panch bhutas, i.e. 5 basic elements). The whole universe, along with its all life forms are, then, made with various permutation and combination of all these elements and 'Mana'. This evolution has been shown in Fig 4.2, which is self-explanatory. (Refer to Sec.4.6.3 for pure consciousness.)

The creation by Lord Brahma (who Himself was created from Maha-Tattva), is given in next para.

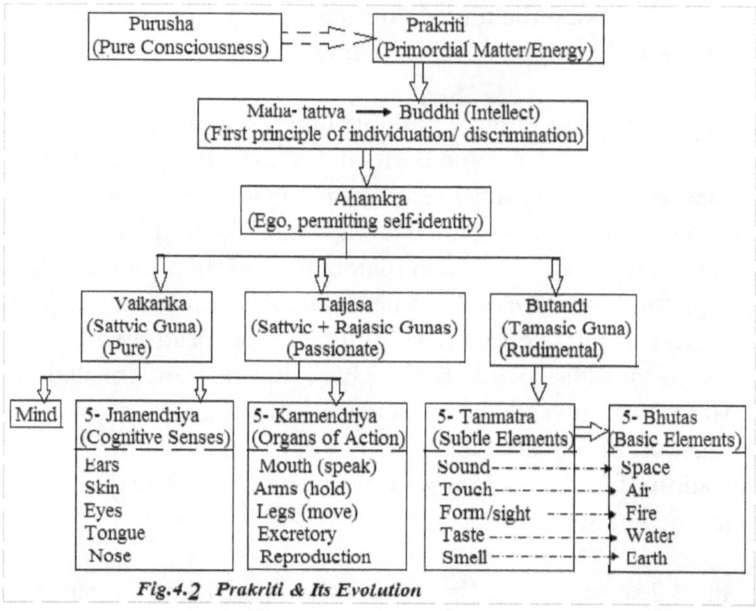

Fig.4.2 Prakriti & Its Evolution

The earlier mentioned theory of 'expansion and contraction' is, often, presented little differently as "Theory of Evolution & Involution". In first, i.e. evolution phase, the soul consciousness (as a part of Maha-Vishnu) descends and / or expands first into subtle matter or subtle energy and then into gross matter or gross energy. The soul consciousness, then, enters into gross physical bodies and later, as per wish of Maha-Vishnu, the second phase (the phase of involution) begins. In this phase the soul gradually withdraws from the gross physical body into the inner subtle bodies and finally into Itself (Maha-Vishnu). At the individual level, the first phase usually involves the Soul (Atman) becoming jivatma by getting caught in the web of samsara (phenomenal world) and developing attachment with the sense objects through the play of the triple gunas (sattva, rajas and tamas) and the activity of the senses. In the second phase the jivatma develop detachment, withdraw their senses into their minds and their minds into their subtle planes and inner states of consciousness through yoga /meditation and other contemplative processes and finally experience oneness with their true consciousness (Maha-Vishnu) in a state of samadhi.

In brief, we can say that human beings are composed of not just of one thing, matter, but of three things, sthula (matter), manas (mind), and atman (spirit). Our true self is Atman and not the Body or Mind. Again, it is said that during 'Pralaya' or 'Maha-pralaya', only the physical bodies (matter and mind) get destroyed/ dissolved and the spirit Atman) goes back in Maha-Vishnu and reappears, as per the wish of Maha-Vishnu, in some form or other during next creation.

4.7.2   Stages of Creation of universe

Given below are the nine steps of the creation of universe, including all life forms, as per Hindu mythology. First three steps are "Prakritik Stage" as they are created naturally (i.e. by Prakriti) by the wish of Maha-Vishnu. Rest six stages are said to be created by Lord Brahma—

1- Creation of Maha-Tattva, Buddhi, Ahamkara, in its three types as already discussed and shown in Fig.4.2.

2- Creation of Tanmatras (subtle elements) and panch-bhutas (basic elements) -- Bhutadi Ego distorted into fundamental of sound, of which 'Ether' (space) was produced. Thus, sound is characteristics of Ether (space). Then Ether, with its sound became productive and caused fundamental of touch, from which 'Wind (Air)' was originated. Then touch and wind became productive and produced the fundamental of 'Form/sight (color)', which caused 'Fire (light)'. Fire (light) becoming productive produced the characteristic of taste from which originated 'Water' with taste characteristic. Then water deformed and created characteristics of smell of which "Earth" originated with smell as its property. These Five Basic Elements (also called as "Panch-Mahabhuta") are elemental creations, proceeding from the principle of Egotism affected by the property of Darkness.

3- Creation of 'mind' from Vaikarika Ego and Dasendria
    (10 organs) from Taijasa Ego, i.e. 5 cognitive senses and
    5 organs of action, as shown in Fig. 4.2.

4- Mukhya (Main) Creation Stage- After the three Prakritik
    Stages, Lord Brahma, thru meditation, created
    immovable objects like Planets, Mountains with five
    types of Vegetation's (trees, shrubs, climbing plants,
    creepers and grasses), which lacks the ability like intellect,
    sense of motion etc.

5- Animal Creation (Tiryak) Stage- Brahma, then, meditated
    again and there appeared animals with over 28 different
    types, their characteristic was the quality of darkness,
    poor in knowledge and wisdom and mistaking error etc.
    This, to some extent, validates Darwin's theory that
    animals evolved before human and human being are
    refined form of animals.

6- Divinity (immortals) Creation (Urddhasrotas) stage-
    Unhappy with his previous creations Lord Brahma
    started meditating again and a third creation appeared,
    abounding with the quality of goodness, who were
    endowed with pleasure and enjoyment, unburdened
    internally or externally, and luminous within and without.
    Main, as per sequence, were the followings-

    a- Four Sankadi Rishis (4 Kumaras)- First appeared
        from Brahma's mind (born from mind)
         four Kumaras, named Sanaka, Sanatana, Sanandana
        and Sanatkumara. They were born infant, who lacked
        the feeling of desire and they thought they are
        incapable of giving birth to mankind, hence refused
        to proceed with the order of Brahma and instead
        devoted themselves to Lord Vishnu and undertook
        lifelong vows of renunciation & celibacy. They
        studied Vedas from their childhood and remained in
        the form of children due to their spiritual virtues.

b- Rudras- As Kumaras didn't agree for creation,
    Brahma got so frustrated and angry that a crying
    baby Rudra appeared from his forehead. However,
    Rudra too decided to follow the path of Penance and
    Brahma was again disappointed. After a lot of
    cajoling by Brahma, Rudra agreed to help and
    manifested 10 more beings with the same appearance
    as him. These are known as the 11 Rudras, one of
    whom is said to be Lord Shiva.

c- Ten Prajapatis- Brahma, then, thought that to desire
    anything, knowledge is essential. So, he decided that
    knowledge should be present before the birth of
    mankind. As such, He, from His mind, created seven
    sons (Manas Putras), often called as "Saptarishi"
    (Vashista, Krathu, Pulasthya, Pulaha, Angirasa, Atri
    & Marichi). These seven Divine Sage were born with
    highest divine knowledge, clairvoyance, very long life
    & for the purpose to spread religion & knowledge
    and, to fulfil these purposes, they performed penance
    and became 'Brahmarishi' (highest class of rishis who
    has understood the meaning of Brahman). Later
    Brahma created three more sons in sage form
    (Prachetasa, Bhrigu and Narada). Some scriptures
    call these 10 sons as 10 Prajapatis (Lord of creature)
    and all possess Brahma Gyan and unique qualities.
    However, the names of Saptarishis of present
    manvantara are slightly different.

d- When all these sons refused to get entangled in the
    process of procreation, Brahma got filled up with
    negative energy - this resulted in the creation
    of Asuras / Demons. However, when Brahma again
    focused on his positive energy, many Devas / Demi-
    gods emerged.

e- Lord Brahma continued creating many more sons /
    personalities from different parts of His body, some
    of those are called as different demi-gods. Daksha

(known as Daksha Prajapati) is known as First
Prajapati (off course after Brahma himself) who,
later, married to "Prasuti" (daughter of Svayambhuva
Manu and Shatrupa) and that is known as first
marriage in Hinduism.

7- Manushya (Mankind) Stage- After creating so many
divine personalities, Lord Brahma thought of giving birth
to human race and created a lookalike of himself, a male,
named "Manu" (often called Swayambhu Manu) and also
a female named "Shatarupa" (meaning one who can take
multiple forms). Shatarupa became wife of Manu and
they both gave birth to two sons named
Priyavrata and Uttanapada and three daughters, named
Prasuti, Aakuti and Devahuti. Two of the daughters of
Prasuti were Aditi and Diti and both were married to
Rishi Kashyap. Aditi gave birth to most Demi-gods and,
also, Vaivasvata Manu who's descendent became present
mankind. Refer to next section and Fig.4.3.

Biblical counter parts for Manu and Shatarupa can be
said as Adam and Eve, with minor difference as Adam
was directly created by God and Eve was created from
Adam's rib, but Manu and Shatarupa, both, self-emerged
from Brahma. Similar counter parts in Islam are Aadam
and Hawwa.

One legend says that after Manu and Shatarupa were
told by Brahma to populate the Earth with their progeny,
the planet Earth, which was created earlier by Brahma
could not be located. A demon called Hiranyaksh (the
Golden-Eyed), had abducted the Earth
(goddess Bhumi) from her central position in Bhu-loka
and imprisoned her in the lower planetary system
of Rasaatal (lower portion of Cosmic Ocean known as
Garbhodak). As per request of Brahma, Lord Vishnu
incarnated the form of a huge boar (Varaha) to perform
the dual task of releasing Bhumi-devi from
imprisonment and vanquishing the demon Hiranyaksh.

Though Varaha Avatar is actually the third Avatar of Vishnu, it was Vishnu's first avatar in the present day of Brahma and the previous two avatars occurred earlier. After the Earth was restored, Manu and Shatarupa took change of its affairs.

8- Anugraha (Minor Divinity) Creation Stage- Lord Brahma also created other class with little divine powers, i.e. possesses both the qualities of goodness and darkness, like Yakshas (nature spirit who are benevolent, and custodians of treasures, though sometimes mischievous), Pisachas (goblins), Gandharva (singers & musicians), Apsaras (nymphs of heaven), Sarapas (Serpent), Kinnaras (beings with the heads of horses) etc.

9- Last Stage- In the final Ninth Stage, the four divine Sankadi Rishis (4-Kumaras) reappeared to enlighten the world with their knowledge, wisdom and guidance. It is said that 4-Kumara creation is both primary and secondary.

Brahma also sprouted the four Vedas from his mouth and created such things as Dharma (righteousness or truth) and Adharma (un-truth). Thus, the creation of universe by Lord Brahma was over as He has successfully built a platform for regeneration work to happen by itself and that is going on and on till date. To oversee His creation during creation stage, Brahma had made His head four-faced to look in all four directions at the same time. Some scripture says that after creation of universe, Brahma became extremely proud and started thinking Himself as sole owner and controller of the universe and 'Prakriti' and sprouted his fifth head as 'Ego'. Lord Shiva, then, cutoff Brahma's fifth head (Ego) and Brahma remained neutral (neither feared not wanted to control His creation and Prakriti). Prakriti (Creation) was left to follow her own natural course and obey her own natural laws.

Another minor variation of creation by Brahma is that first Brahma split Himself and created a lady form, Goddess Shatarupa. Her beauty captivated Brahma, and he desired to possess her. Shatarupa can acquire hundred beautiful forms. So, each time Brahma desired to possess her, she changed herself to another form. Thus, she turned into a cow, a mare, a goose, a doe and so on. Lord Brahma kept pursuing her, taking the form of the corresponding male - a bull, a horse, a gander, a buck and so on. Thus, all creatures of the cosmos, from the smallest insect to the largest mammal, came into being.

4.7.3   Origin of present Humankind

Presented here is a very simplified version of origin of present Humankind (mankind). As stated, Brahma created many sons (born from mind or various parts of body) and one lookalike Swayambhu Manu and a female consort, Shatarupa. Shatarupa married Swayambhuva Manu and had five children — two sons, Priyavrata and Uttānapāda, and three daughters, Ākūti, Devahūti and Prasuti. Prasuti married Daksha and they had 16 daughters of which two were Aditi and Diti. Devahuti married Kardama, another mind-born son of Brahma, and they had a son, Lord Kapila, and nine daughters, of which one was Kala. Kala was married to another Brahma's son, Rishi Marichi and they had a son, Kashyap. Aditi and Diti, both were married to Kashyap. Ofcourse Kashyap had few other wives also. Diti gave birth to demons Hiranyakashipu and Hiranyaksha etc. and few Maruts. Aditi gave birth to Vivasvan (an Aditya) and other Adityas (celestial deities) and Demi-gods. Vivasvan is also known as Surya (the Sun God of 7th Manu) and Vivasat. Vivasvan (with wife Samjna) had a son named Vaivasvata Manu. Refer to Family Tree up-to Lava-Kusha, in Fig.4.3.

Vaivasvata Manu is the seventh (and current) Manu. Legends say that in each day of Brahma (i.e. Kalpa), there are 14 Manvantaras (duration or lifespan of a Manu) and each Manvantara is created and ruled by a specific Manu. As such, there are 14 Manus. (Refer Fig.5.1). We can say that 'Manu' is, actually, not a name but title for the creator of each

'Manvantara'. The first Manu was Swayambhu Manu. Our present Humankind is in seventh Manvantara and current Manu is called Vaivasvata Manu. He is also known as Sraddhadeva (as his wife's name was Sraddha), King Satyavrata or Vaivasvata (son of Vivasvan). Vaivasvata had ten sons. One, named Iksvaku, started the Solar dynasty (Suryavansh, also known as Iksvaku dynasty), and another, named Ila, started Lunar dynasty (Chandravansh). Iksvaku had 100 sons. The eldest one, Vikukshi, developed Suryavansh and another son, Nimi, founded Videha dynasty (King Janak and Sita). Descendants of Vikukshi continued one after another (few notables ones are Harishchandra, Bharata, Sagar, Dilipa, Bhagirath, Ambarisha, Raghu, Ajan) up-to Dasharatha and Lord Rama.

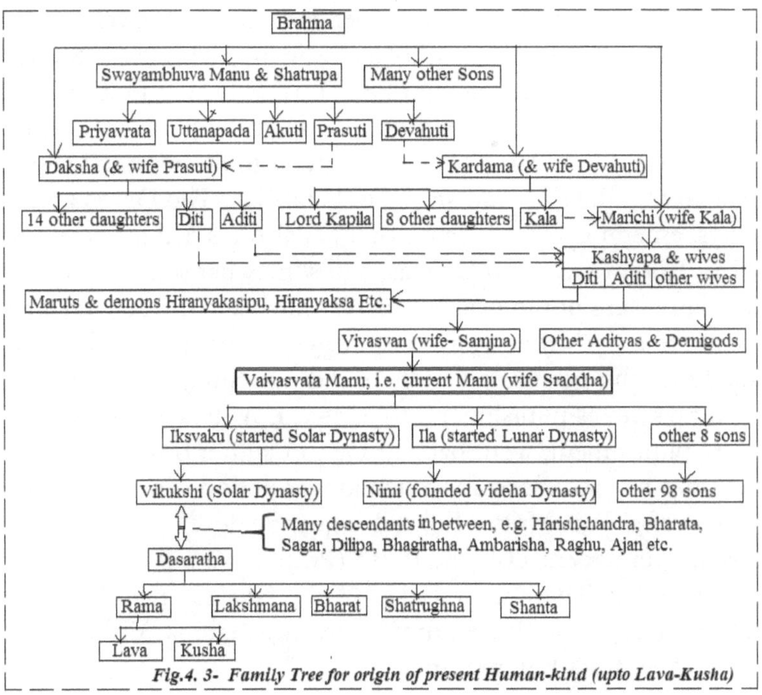

Fig.4. 3- Family Tree for origin of present Human-kind (upto Lava-Kusha)

Many other stories tell little differently about the Humankind on Earth. One says that Priyavrata, son of Swayambhu Manu, established domain over Mortal Realm. Seven of his sons became the ruler of seven Mortal Realms (7 big Islands / planets). One of the sons, King Agnidhra, became the king of Jambudvipa (our planet Earth, as an island in Cosmic Ocean). His descendants were Nabhi, Lord Rishabhadeva, Bharath (not the Bharath, son of King Dushyant) and Maharaj Gaya. The area of Jambudvipa, ruled by this Bharath, was called Bhaaratvarsha (India). Another story says that Rishi Atri (Brahma's son) married Anasuya (daughter of Kardama and Devahuti) and one of their descendants was King Dushyant, whose son was Bharath. This Bharath was the ancestor of Pandavas and Kauravas of Mahabharata. Thus, the Humankind developed from different ancestors and settled at different places. Their race, color, culture etc. became different, depending on geographic locations, climates and vested interests etc.

As per yet another story / legend, earlier the supreme Power had created only two Lokas (residential abodes)—Swarg-Lok or Dev-Lok (Heaven) and Patal Lok or Danav-Lok or Narak-Lok (Hell). Sons/children of Aditi became Devas (Deities / Gods) stayed in Dev-Lok and children of Diti became Daityas / Danavas / Rakshas and stayed in Patal Lok. The Devas and Daitys, emerging directly from Brahma also resided in these two Lokas. Both, Devas and Daityas, had somewhat supernatural life spans and were not in cycle of regular birth and death. But, later a separate Lok (Mrityu-Lok) was created so that the residents of Dev-Lok, who performed badly or did something grossly wrong, could be sent, as punishment, to Mrityu-Lok. Few with less severe punishment, went back to Dev-Lok after one birth-death cycle, but few remained for much longer period with many birth-death cycles. This Mrityu-Lok subsequently developed into a separate permanent Lok, the Earth (Prithvi) we call it today and we live in that. These three Lokas (Trilok) do not include the abodes of Supreme Power, the Trinity, i.e. Brahma, Vishnu & Shiva. They are 'Omnipresent'.

This theory of formation of Mrityu-Lok can have crude analogy as development of country Australia. Earlier the convicts from England were sent to the then un-inhabited country Australia, as punishment. Few, with shorter span of punishment, were allowed to go back to England, but rest had to stay there permanently. This, subsequently, led to development of Australia as a separate country.

Few scriptures mention that 'Patal Lok' is not a separate Lok but is the underground of Bhur Lok (Earth). They clarify the 'Trilok' (three Lok) concept by esoterically referring to as three-dimensional Earth planes---

1- 1ˢᵗ is 'Physical plane' (Bhur Lok) and is clearly visible, consisting of physical bodies of human, animals, materials etc. It is the dense material plane in which all living bodies grow according to its rules and regulations and have their own consciousness.

2- 2ⁿᵈ one is 'Astral plane' or 'etheric plane' (Bhuvar Lok or Bhava Lok) is a magnetic field of emotions and feelings and plays an important role in the desire / mind of most human being. Some say that people who die without their intense desire being filled up, don't get liberated and their soul remains in this Lok and, sometime, they appear in some shape as ghosts. Few say that this is sort of punishment for that soul, before the soul is either reborn in physical plane (Bhur Lok) or gets liberated and goes to next Lok (say Swarg Lok). Though not a true analogy, it may have some similarity with Patal Lok (Hell) mentioned above.

3- The 3ʳᵈ plane is 'Mental plane' cum 'Spiritual plane' (Swarg Lok or Svah). It is sort of gaseous electric plane of mental thought formation, including consciousness, personality, spiritual visions and awareness towards divine power. Enlightened person can go to "Higher Self". (Also refer Sec.2.1.2)

4.7.4   Darwinian theory vis-à-vis Hinduism Philosophy

Though, in absence of more acceptable theory, Darwin's theory is accepted by many, there are many critics also. It was put forward as an imaginary hypothesis in the context of the primitive scientific understanding of the nineteenth century, and, till today, it has not been validated by any scientific discovery or experiment. Today, branches of science such as paleontology, genetics, biochemistry, and molecular biology have proven that it is quite impossible for life to come about as a result of chance and to emerge by itself from natural conditions. Without going into debate, some of the points, which negate the Darwin's Theory, are given below-

1- Consciousness doesn't come from a combination of chemicals. Consciousness is a nonmaterial energy.

2- If evolution meant gradual genetic change within a species, we'd have only one species today— a single highly evolved descendant of the first species. Yet we have many… How does this diversity arise from one ancestral form?

3- Again, if evolution takes millions and millions of years, we should still be able to see some stages of its process. But we simply don't observe any partially evolved fish, lizards, birds, dogs, cats among us. Every species of plant and animal is complete and fully formed.

4- If the theory is true, we should be able to find examples of species that link together major groups suspected to have common ancestry, like birds with reptiles and fish with amphibians.

5- It is only a theory, not a scientific law--- it is not testable or verifiable.

6- If humans descended from monkeys, why are there still monkeys?

7- Don't dinosaurs contradict the "from simple to complex forms" or "from small to big" concept?

8- The fossil record shows us that man came into existence millions of years ago in just the same form as he is now.

As mentioned earlier, Darwin's theory of life emerging on Earth is called a 'process of evolution', but the Vedic / Hindu concept of life on Earth is a 'process of inverse evolution'. Hinduism presents this theory of evolution differently. It is not that so-called modern intelligence has developed by the gradual process of evolution. In the beginning of creation there was a very intelligent personality, Lord Brahma, and from him intelligence and knowledge permeated to all his sons and creations. Even they, in-spite of their great education and knowledge, cannot actually understand the perfection of the living entity's relationship with supreme power, say Maha-Vishnu. As stated in Puranas, there is a gradual evolutionary process, but it is not the body that is evolving. The humanity is always present. The concept of evolution is confined to spiritual evolution. All the bodily forms are already there. It is the spiritual entity, or spiritual spark within the body, that is being promoted by the laws of nature under the supervision of superior authority. As said earlier, from the very beginning of creation different varieties of living entities were existing. It is not that some of them have become extinct. Everything is there; it is due to our lack of knowledge and vision that we cannot see things in their proper perspective. The Supreme Power, say Maha-Vishnu, can be understood, not by advanced knowledge, but by pure transcendental and devotional service.

As stated above, Hinduism, in general, believe life on earth coming as "process of Invert Evolution", i.e. life coming from top, as opposed to Darwin's "Process of Evolution", i.e. life developing from bottom. However, few Hindus lend some support of Darwin's theory by citing example of Dashavatar (10 Incarnations of Lord Vishnu), how Vishnu appeared as 'Avatars' sequence-wise from simple life-forms to more complex, i.e. from fish to present human. Though 10 Avatars will be discussed further in next chapter, the analogy given below lends some support to Darwin's theory.

1- Matasya (Fish) Avatar tells that first the first-class of vertebrates, like fish, evolved in water.

2- Kurma (Turtle) Avatar tells that some of the sea vertebrates moved out of water and became amphibious (living in both water and land), like turtle.

3- Varaha (Boar) Avatar tells that some of the amphibious developed into mammal wild land animal. Similar to appearance of Dinosaurs.

4- Narasimha Avatar depicts that some animals got developed in part human form, i.e. part animal and part human. This also indicates emergence of human thoughts and intelligence in powerful wild nature.

5- Vamana Avatar indicates that some of the animals developed into short and premature human being i.e. midgets who couldn't grow tall. We may also consider this as transition from Homo Erectus (a species of archaic humans that lived throughout most of the Pleistocene geological epoch) to Homo Sapiens (scientific name for the present human species).

6- Parasurama Avatar depicts early humans living in forests and using weapons and not social.

7- Rama Avatar indicates humans as rational thinking social being, who practiced and laid out the laws of society and started living in organized community.

8- Balarama Avatar tells human showing great interest in agriculture.

9- Krishna Avatar depicts humans practicing animal husbandry and development of politically and diplomatically advanced societies. Also, development of skills to live and thrive in the adharmic (unrighteousness) social structure.

10- Kalki Avatar (yet to come) indicates advanced humans with great powers of destruction.

4.8   How Universe was created (other Mythologies lens)

Most of the cultures / mythologies agree that this universe is created by God, Brahman, Maha Vishnu, Allah, Pangu or Izanagi, whatever we may call Him, only the presentation varies. Even the Australian Aborigines, which are likely the oldest tribe on our planet, with a known continuity of cultural history going back to over 50,000 years, speak of the "Dreamtime" of the distant past when the Gods walked on the Earth and created people, sacred places, animals and the ways of human society. Only few cultures, like Jainism, hold that the world, souls and time are uncreated, unbeginning and unending.

As per the Boshongo People of central Africa, in the beginning there was only darkness, water, and the great god Bumba. One day Bumba, in pain from a stomachache, vomited up the sun. In time the sun dried up some of the water, leaving land. But Bumba was still in pain and vomited some more. Up came the moon, the stars, and then some animals (e.g. the leopard, the crocodile, the turtle), and finally man.

As per the Mayans of Mexico and Central America, before creation there existed only the sea, the sky, and the 'Maker'. The Maker, unhappy because there was no one to praise him, created the earth, mountains, trees, and most animals. But the animals could not speak, and so he decided to create humans. He initiated making human with many materials but was not satisfied, till finally he made human with white and yellow corn, which came to His satisfaction.

In traditional Chinese mythology, Pangu can be interpreted as creator deity. In the beginning there was nothing and Pangu was resting in cosmic egg. Because of some setting of 'Yin' and 'Yang' energies, Pangu emerged (woke up) from the cosmic egg. He separated Yin from Yang with a swing of his giant axe, creating the Earth (murky Yin) and the Sky (clear Yang). To keep them separated, Pangu stood between them and pushed up the Sky. This task took eighteen thousand years, with each day the sky grew ten feet higher, the Earth ten feet wider, and Pangu ten feet taller. In some versions of the story, Pangu is aided in this task by the four most prominent creatures, namely the Turtle, the Qilin, the Phoenix, and the Dragon.

As per Bible, God created the universe, including Earth in distant past. His creation time was six days, but His days were not the human days of 24 hours but much longer, could have been thousands of years. God did not make life in a simple form and allow it to evolve into more complex forms. Instead, he created basic "kinds" of complex plants and animals, which then reproduced "according to their kinds." God's sequence of creation was as below. If we observe closely, the sequence of creation is not much different from the sequence/ steps mentioned earlier in Sec.4.7.2 (Hindu Mythology).

1- On 1st day, God created the universe, including Earth. The Earth was formless, desolate and totally dark as the raging ocean covered everything. God, then, commanded, "Let there be light"—and light appeared. God then separated the light from the darkness, and He named the light "Day" and the darkness "Night." (refer Mukhya Creation stage and earlier of Sec.4.7.2).

2- The earth was covered with water and a dense mantle of vapor. On 2nd day, God separated these two elements, creating a gap between the watery surface and the canopy of vapor. The dome-like vapory portion was termed as 'Sky' or 'Heaven'. (refer Mukhya Creation stage and earlier of Sec.4.7.2).

3- On 3rd day, as commanded by God, water under the sky gathered at one portion and dry land appeared at another portion. He named the land as 'Earth' and the water as 'Sea'. As desired by God, more sunlight reached the ground. Some vegetation appeared, with new species started sprouting through the third and subsequent creative days. (refer Mukhya Creation stage of Sec.4.7.2).

4- On 4th day, for better lighting of Earth, God created two large lights, the Sun to rule the day and the moon to rule the night. God also created many stars to shine for same purpose. (refer Divinity Creation and minor Divinity creation stages of Sec.4.7.2).

5- On the 5th day, God created underwater creatures and flying creatures in great numbers with the ability to procreate within their kinds. (refer to animal creation stage of Sec.4.7.2).

6- On 6th day, God created land animals, both large and small and lastly, God created human beings, making them to be like himself. He created them as male and female, blessed them, and said them to procreate and take charge of all the fish, birds, animals and vegetation etc. and, thus, God's creation was complete. (refer to animal creation stage and Manushya creation stage of Sec.4.7.2).

7- 7th day, called as 'Sabbath', after completing the creation, God rested. This gives a message to human-being that "Six days you shall labor, and do all your work, but the seventh day you should rest".

The basic Islamic concept is that God, called Allah, is eternal and self-existent and He created the entire universe and He is the Lord and Sovereign of the Universe. Islam also says that Allah created the universe in six days, each day being a very long period of time. This appears somewhat similar to Bible's view, with some differences.

4.8.1   Hindu Mythology vis-à-vis other mythologies

Though we may call Him by different names in different religions / cultures, the creator of our universe is one and only one, that supreme power or ultimate reality, and, as such, there has to be considerable similarities in creation theories of different religions / cultures. Just for example, few similarities are given below ---

1- Similarity of creation theory of Hinduism (Sec.4.7.2) and Christianity and Islamic theories (Sec.4.8).

2- As it appears, Brahma's Creation closely follows actual appearance of elements in our universe-- first to appear are the intangible elements like the protons, neutrons etc. (the three Gunas & Maha- Tattva), followed by matter in gaseous form; followed by the immovable planets and landmasses; then the vegetation; birds, aquatics and animals; and finally, the Higher species. Also, the mode of reproduction is clearly "Nonsexual" in the beginning (as seen with the generation of Rudras and Rudranis, the female principles of Rudras, or Manu and Shatarupa) and becomes "sexual- intercourse" only after the germination of Daksha and his consort Prasuti. This somewhat validates the Adam & Eve or Aaadam & Hawwa, who were initially non-sexual.

3- 'Manu' is the root-word for both, the Sanskrit 'Manushya' and the English 'Man'. The word 'Man' derives origin from the Germanic 'Mannus', which stems from the same root as Manu.

4- The appearance of first Manu, Svayambhuva Manu and Shatarupa, on Earth is, somewhat similar to appearance of Adam and Eve (Christianity) or Aaadam and Hawwa (Islam), or Mashya and Mashyana (Zoroastrian Mythology) or Ask and Embla (Norse mythology) on Earth. First man, Swayambhu Manu was born (on his own) with the 'Kaya' (shape) of his father Brahma.

Similarly, Bible says - 'Man was created in the image of his Maker, God'.

5- The seventh and current Manu (Vaivasvata Manu) is also known as 'Jal-plavan-Manu', i.e., 'Manu of the Great Deluge'. There are some similarities in the stories of Manu and Noah (Christianity- Old Testaments). In these stories both Manu and Noah, in the company of others, survived a great flood on a watercraft, a very long time ago. As per Matsya Avatar, Manu (King Satyavrata) saved the necessary lives, from the Great Deluge (Pralaya), for starting next Manu creation, by making a big boat and carrying all necessary lives, with the help of Vishnu's incarnated fish. Similarly, as per the story of Noah from the Old Testament book of Genesis, God became very angry of humans He had made, for they had become very wicked and violent. He decided to destroy them, but save the blameless Noah and his sons, and instructed Noah to build a three-story ark, to hold them, their wives and children, and a male and female of various animals, cattle, fowl, creeping things, along with provisions for them. After that, the great flood / deluge occurred, destroying most of the things, but saved and grounded the ark safely on a mountain range.

Islam's Qur'an also has references to Noah and declares that he received a revelation to build an Ark, after his people refused to believe in his message and hear the warning. In Greek Mythology, Deucalion is forewarned of the flood and he builds an ark and staffs it with creatures. Many other cultures have flood stories similar to those. They tend to be simpler and less detailed than the ancient flood stories mentioned above. From scientific angle, The Ark carrying Manu / Noah / Deucalion and other survivors would have been guided by the global currents generated by the melting waters.

4.9   How Corporation is created

For creation of universe, we had presumed that the Board of Directors, Chairman and CEO were all in one, i.e. Brahman, the Supreme Power, the Ultimate Reality and He has taken care of everything from His infinite energy and resources and He has designated (taken form of) Brahma as the creator of the universe. In the same way, we will presume that for the concerned corporate entity, the type of business, the Board of Directors, Chairman or CEO have been decided and other formalities, few of those mentioned below, have been done.

- i-   Finalizing corporation name & articles of incorporation,
- ii- Appointing initial directors and, later, Board of Directors
- iii- Issuing stocks and shares
- iv- Securities registration and exemptions
- v-   Tax & Insurance formalities
- vi- Obtaining licenses and permits
- vii- Opening Corporate Bank accounts etc.

After above mentioned incorporation actions have been done and the Chairman / CEO has appointed I/c Planning & Project for creation of that corporate entity, the I/c Planning & Project takes over and works on following areas/divisions started one after another or concurrently, as per need and necessary area / divisional heads are also appointed. It is presumed that conceptualization, i.e. feasibility, concept of product and rough process have already been decided by the Chairman and the Board.

- 1- Specification of the equipment and systems finalization, including reliability & maintainability of the equipment / systems.
- 2- Publication, information and broadcasting,
- 3- Design of equipment and systems, taking care of safety of men & equipment and environment and also standardization & variety reduction. Reliability and maintainability factors, in relation to equipment

performance, should also be considered. Rough financial evaluation of the design to be done to ensure economic viability.

4- Manufacturing of equipment and systems, including quality control and proper inputs; both, onsite and offsite (contractor's premises). Design fault, if any, should also be considered.

5- Making / arranging infrastructures (buildings, roads, power, fuel, water, air etc.) and other necessary logistics / facilities.

6- Erection and installation of equipment and systems, correcting any minor design defects and ensuring maintainability for most of the anticipated maintenance problems (mainly on logistics).

7- Testing & commissioning, including correcting minor design defects and installation defects. This also includes handing over to operating personnel and necessary on-job training.

Refer to Sec.4.11 and Sec.5.3 also. We would not go into details of these as theme of the book is governance of universe and not of any corporate entity.

4.10   Organization of Creator, Lord Brahma

It has been discussed earlier that Lord Brahma, the creator of universe, is called 'Hiranyagarbha', Svayambhu (self-born) and Vagisa (Lord of Speech). He is also known as Prajapati (Lord of creatures) Brahma and Pitamaha (the father of fathers) etc. As a creator, he can be called a Cosmic Engineer. We have already discussed the two versions of his appearance (not exactly birth). He is shown seated either in Yoga's Sukhasana pose or on a lotus flower or on a hamsa (swan). Hamsa stands for wisdom and prejudice and his chariot is driven by hamsas. His wife / consort is Goddess Saraswathi. Please refer back to Sec.3.1 for more about Brahma and Saraswathi.

Brahma is not only a creator, but also a great spiritual teacher. Many Vedic seers were his mind born children, who later recomposed the Vedas and taught Vedas and Upanishads to serious students.

4.10.1   Prerequisites of the creator

Brahma appears like an old man, with four bearded faces, that look in four directions at the same time for creating and monitoring jobs. This also symbolize that Lord Brahma is the omni-present and the omnipotent. The white beard on each face suggests to his old age and wisdom and the long beard indicates that creation is a never-ending process. The crown on his head implies that he has the supreme power and authority over the process of creation. He is shown in a meditative mood. Brahma's four faces (four head) also represent four Vedas and four Maha-Yugas. He has four arms, holding following things for different purposes, (see Fig.4.4)

1- Pustak (book) in one hand- The book represents Brahma holding the Vedas in one hand, which symbolizes knowledge in the world which is important for creation.

2- Water pot in second hand- The whole Universe evolves out of water, so Lord Brahma carries water in the water pot. Water pot is also used in the prayer ritual (Kamandalu) and it symbolize the cosmic energy which helps for creation and existence of the universe.

3- Lotus flower in third hand- Lotus symbolizes purity, fertility and non-attachments (Louts flower represents the nature and all -encompassing energy of creation). It also represents that Brahma appeared from Maha-Vishnu's naval, sitting on lotus.

4- Rosary (beaded Mala) in fourth hand- It is used to aid in meditation that symbolize all the substances that go into the creating the universe and also to keep track of the universe's time.

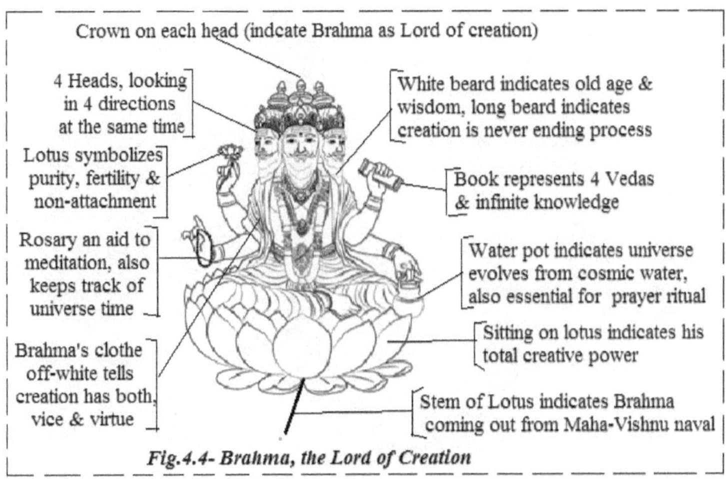

Fig.4.4- Brahma, the Lord of Creation

As creation is the work of the mind and the intellect, Lord Brahma symbolizes the Universal Mind. Qualities of Brahma, for creation, may be considered as 'truth', 'consciousness', 'bliss', 'beyond ego', 'beyond qualities', 'infinite' and 'subtler than the subtlest' etc. His abode is said as 'Brahmaloka'. Brahma's clothes, that are off-white, represents the dual nature of creation, that is purity and impurity, happiness and unhappiness, vice and virtue, knowledge and ignorance etc. (Modern psychology and science also say that apparent opposites, like good & bad or hot & cold or vice & virtue, can't exist without each other; it is similar to principle of complementarity.) Brahma sitting or standing on a lotus indicates that he represents the creative power of the Supreme Reality.

Lord Brahma had one problem… He couldn't refuse any boon (except immortality) to anyone or any demon, whosoever pleased him by worshiping. In that process, he sometime gave serious destructive power to few demons. When those demons started creating serious problems to others, it was left to Lord Vishnu, the preserver, or sometime Lord Shiva, the destroyer, to find ways to destroy those demons. It is similar to industrial corporation situation, when, because of some poor project creation quality, some problem comes up at use stage, the I/c Preservation and Production has to rectify that.

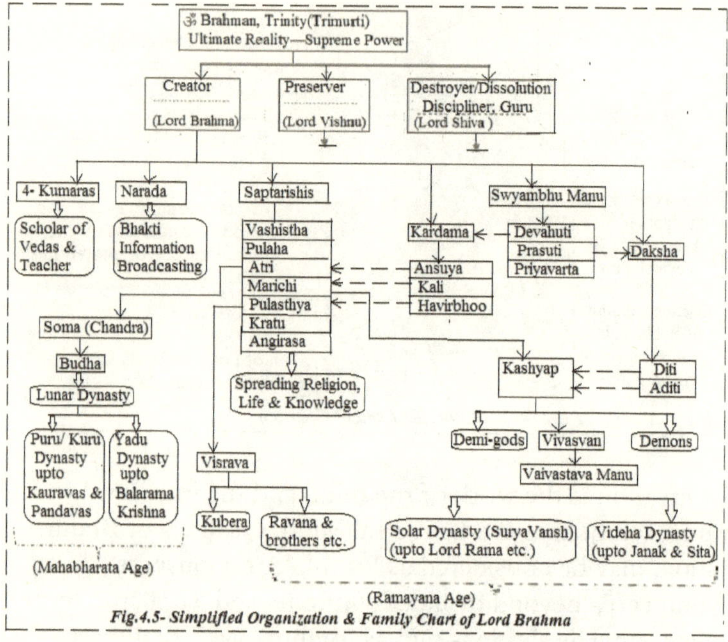

Fig.4.5- Simplifled Organization & Family Chart of Lord Brahma

4.10.2 Organization Chart for Brahma's Creation

Fig.4.3 shows the Brahma's creation only for present humankind, but organization chart for Brahma's total creation is roughly shown in Fig.4.5. The figure shows how Brahma's created sons helped Brahma in further creation and procreation. For simplicity, the figure only gives the relevant off-springs of individuals, though there may be many more off-springs of those individuals.

For creation of any big industrial corporation, first the chief of the project is selected and then the chief selects his team. As the project creation continues, the chief inducts more personnel to continue creation. Somewhat similar way, Brahman, the supreme Power takes the shape of creator Brahma. Then Brahma created sons (mind-born or body-born), who started further creation and procreation. As shown in Fig. 4.5 and also mentioned in Sec. 4.7.2, the 4-Kumaras (Sanaka, Sanatana, Sanandana, and Sanatkumara) didn't like procreation, so their function was studying and propagation of Vedas. Again, Narada didn't like to procreate, so his function was to spread Bhakti and also information and broadcasting. Saptarishi's (7- great sages / rishis) function was spreading religion, life principles and knowledge. Again, many of the Saptarishis, later, took part in creation and procreation. The main function of Swayambhu Manu and Daksha was creation and procreation. As shown in Fig. 4.5, Manu's one daughter, Devahuti was married to rishi Kardama and another, Prasuti was married to Daksha. Three of Kardama's many daughters, Anasuya, Kali and Havirbhoo were married to Brahma's sons, Atri, Marichi and Pulasthya respectively. Two of Daksha's many daughters were married to rishi Kashyap, son of rishi Marichi. Atri's descendants (thru Soma, Budha etc.) started two dynasties- one Puru / Kuru dynasty, leading to Pandavas and Kauravas and another Yadu dynasty, leading to Balarama and Krishna. Marichi's descendants, thru Kashyap, Visavan and Vaivastava Manu, started two dynasties, one Solar Dynasty (Suryavansh), leading to Rama, Lakshmana etc., and another Videha Dynasty, leading to King Janak and Sita. Of-course, another set of sons of Kashyap (thru Diti) became demons and yet another set of Kashyap's sons (thru) Aditi, became Demigods and Adityas. Pulasthya's descendants, thru Visvara, became Kubera and Ravana. Brahma created few other sons for different roles.

Brahma's creation continues, somewhat differently in different Manvantaras and Kalpas.

4.11   Organization of I/c Planning & Project

Apparently, the organization of I/c Planning & Project (Fig.4.6) may look much different from that of Lord Brahma (Fig. 4.5) but going into spirit and considering the different nature of creation, the two may appear reasonably similar. Like Brahma went on creating one after another and his earlier creation assisting Brahma in further creation, I/c Planning & Project goes on from specification to design & development, to manufacturing, to erection and so on and previous creation assisting in subsequent creations. For further details of each created division, please refer back to Sec.4.9.

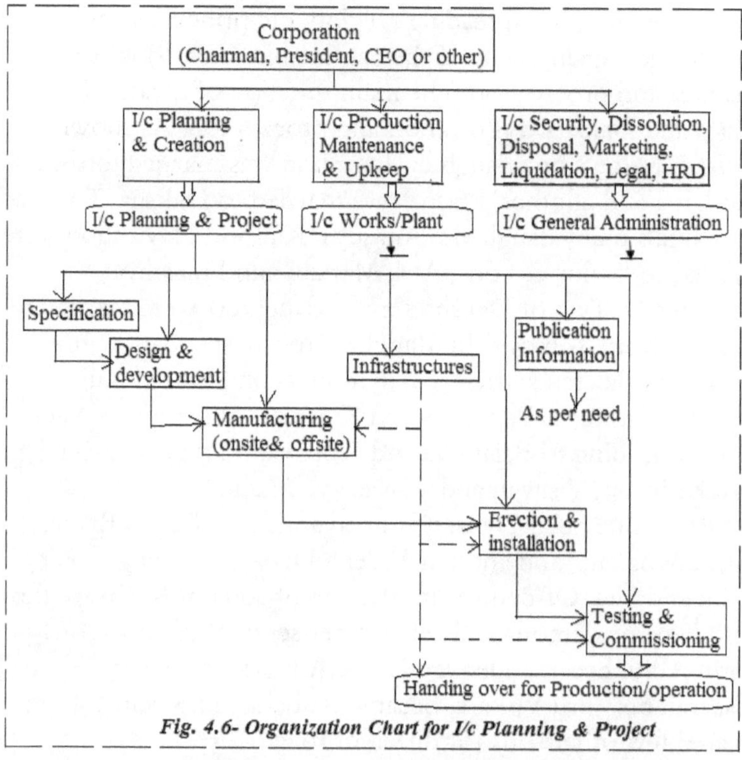

Fig. 4.6- Organization Chart for I/c Planning & Project

4.12   Why Brahma is worshipped less, compared to others

As noted earlier, Brahma, Vishnu and Shiva are the three faces / chiefs of the God (Supreme Power) and are almost equally important and vital for their functions. However, in early Vedic scriptures Brahma is given utmost importance and very little mention of Vishnu and Shiva. But later scriptures give utmost importance to Vishnu, Shiva and Shakti and little significance to Brahma. Also, by virtue of his functions, Brahma seems unapproachable by the mortals, because his duty of creation demands introversion, complete concentration and undivided attention. Therefore, as a personal God he does not have much of an appeal. Probably this is the reason we have extremely few temples of Lord Brahma (about six in all). The most famous and oldest temple of Lord Brahma, in the world, is at Puskar, Rajasthan. In comparison to the 6 temples of Brahma, we have innumerable temples of Vishnu, Shiva and Shakti. However, Brahma is found, as an attendant god in many temples of Vishnu and Shiva. The reasons for so few Brahma temples may be the followings-

1- Our preference for action and war heroes. As said, most of the temples are dedicated to Vishnu, Shiva & Shakti. They are all known for their valor and they pitched battles against evil forces and defeated them. They had weapons like Sudarshan Chakra, Trident, Mace, Sword etc. and could fly and increase their sizes as per need. In contrast, Lord Brahma doesn't depict any fighting action or weapon. We remember Alexander and not Aristotle, Napoleon and not Voltaire and so on. For the same reason, we remember and worship deities like Hanuman, Kartikeya (Murugan), Durga and Kali more as compared to Saraswathi and Brahaspati.

2- Multiple levels of our religious organization. In Hinduism, often, religion applies differently at different levels. Most average people need to be brought into the religion by fear (fear of sin and immorality) and reassurance that the gods will help them tackle their difficulties. The fighting of the gods become a symbolic one against internal fights too. For the mainstream people, gods such as Brahma, or Brahaspathi or Saraswati or Agni don't make much sense and they worship more deities like Vishnu, Shiva, Hanuman, Durga etc. In our society, such people are much more in number as compared to people of higher echelon, such as saints, gurus and other such learned people who knew the religion properly and were not drawn in religion by fear psychosis and fear of sin and handling small problems matter less for them. Big saints meditate on Brahma (the highest of Hindu saints are called the Brahma Rishi) and perform Yajnas invoking Agni. When one elevates in higher planes even the mainstream gods like Vishnu, Shiva, Hanuman etc. become transformed into gods in yogic trance.

3- Understanding of Vedas or Puranas to protect the religion- Vedic people favored Vedic Gods, like Brahma (Prajapati), Agni, Indra etc.in their religion. Rigveda barely mentions Vishnu, Shiva or Shakthi and almost none of Ganesh, Hanuman etc. As Vedas are more philosophical, common men found it hard to related to them. As such, they switched to Puranas, which are far more entertaining and is simple to understand. Lord Brahma didn't find much place in those.

4- Another reason may be that Brahma was directly represented as a Brahmin while other gods spanned all castes. This meant that the later Hindus who realized that this would be a problem in the spread of the religion went for more varna-neutral and non-Vedic Gods (Vishnu, Shiva, Shakti etc.).

5- As mentioned in Sec.4.7.2, after Brahma created the universe, He became extremely proud, considered Himself sole controller of creation and Prakriti and sprouted a fifth head as 'Ego'. Lord Shiva, then, cutoff Brahma's fifth so that Brahma remain neutral. As per another story in this aspect, once there was an argument between Brahma, Vishnu and Shiva as to who is most important. Lord Shiva took the form of a long Linga and told that whosoever sees / touches the both ends of Linga will be considered most important. Vishnu surrendered but Brahma lied and told that he saw. Shiva got angry at Brahma's lie and cutoff Brahma's fifth (Ego) head.

6- Yet another reason can be taken from Sec.4.7.2, which tells that Brahma was so captivated with the beauty of Shatarupa that he wanted to possess her at any cost, even by changing himself to different forms. This shows somewhat poor character.

4.12.1 Why I/c Planning & Project is less important

Similar parallel may be drawn in corporate management. The I/c Project & Planning is solely important during creation of the corporate entity (like Lord Brahma during creation of Universe); but once the entity is created and commissioned, the importance of I/c Project reduces drastically and importance goes to I/c Works (operation & maintenance) and I/c Administration, Security & Justice; in the same way as importance shifts from Lord Brahma to Lord Vishnu and Lord Shiva.

~~~~~~~~~~~~~~~~~~~~~~~~
~~~~~~~~~~~~~~~~~~~~~~~~

5   Preservation aspects of Universe and Corporation

(Ancient India has survived because Hinduism was not developed along material but spiritual lines --- Mahatma Gandhi)

Before we discuss the preservation of universe, we would have a look at how much time preservation is done as compared to creation and dissolution.

5.1   Current Universe Time Division

At the outset, we confess that the data about number of years etc. in coming Fig.5.1 and elsewhere in the book have been taken from different sources, including various free postings on Internet. As such, these may be taken only as indicative and illustrative and genuineness is not confirmed. All years mentioned here are our human years. As said in Sec.2.5, after sleep, Brahma comes out from Maha-Vishnu, creates the universe, the universe keeps going till it is dissolved in Maha-Vishnu and Brahma goes to sleep, before coming out for next universe. This period is called one Brahma Day or Kalpa. In Fig.5.1, we would start with current universe, which is said as 'Varaha Kalpa' and that would last for 4.32 billion years. One Kalpa is divided into 14 Manvantaras (duration of one Manu). Each Manvantara is started by a new Manu and lasts for about 307 million years. We are in 7th Manvantara and our current Manu is Vaivasvata Manu. Each Manvantara is divided into 71 Chatur-Yugas (CY), also known as Divya-Yuga or Maha-Yuga.

We are in 28th Chatur-Yuga (CY-28) and each CY lasts for 4.32 million years. Each Chatur-Yuga is divided into four Yugas,

Satya Yuga (also known as Krita Yuga), Treta Yuga, Dwapara Yuga and Kali Yuga, time period for each given in Fig.5.1. We are, presently, in Kali Yuga. The first Manvantara or first Yuga of a Kalpa starts with major creation by Brahma and the last one of the Kalpa ends with major dissolution. But other Yugas start with partial creation and end with partial destruction / dissolution. Fig.5.1 shows these divisions of ongoing Kali Yuga. The partial creation is called 'Dawn' and the partial dissolution is called 'Dusk' or 'Sandhya' and the in-between period is preservation / sustenance period, which is called 'Main' or 'Day'. Both, the 'Dawn' and 'Dusk' periods are about 9% to 10% of total Kali Yuga time and the 'Main' period is about 80% to 82% of total Kali Yuga time. We are fairly early in Kali Yuga, which started about 5000 years ago and may continue for 427,000 years more.

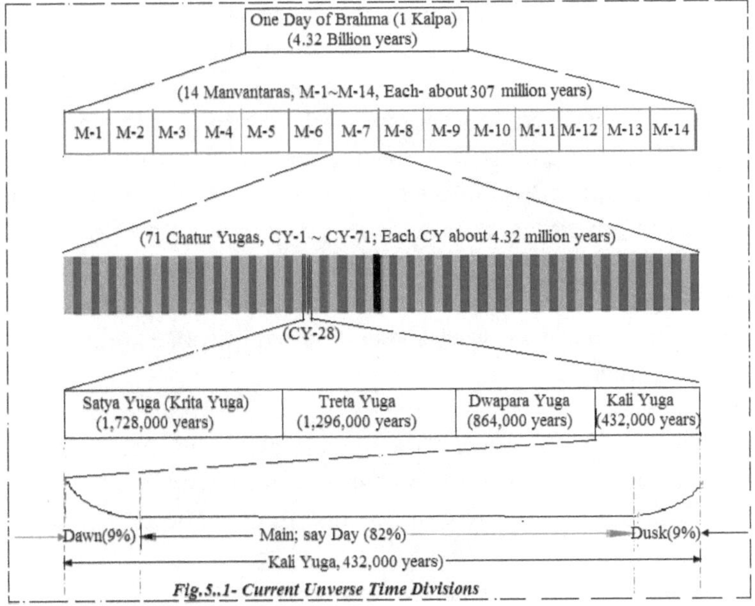

Fig.5..1- Current Unverse Time Divisions

5.2   Need of the Governor during Preservation

Though proper governance is needed for all, creation, preservation and dissolution, it is more necessary for preservation period as that amounts to over 80% of total duration, as seen from Fig. 5.1. For smooth functioning of such long duration of time for Manvantaras, there has to be a governor and his team, i.e. a set of Gods / Devas and guardians for preservation of universe. As in last chapter, here also we would consider the similar three questions, i.e.--

1- 'Who' is responsible for preservation?
2- 'Why' preservation of universe needed?
3- 'How' preservation is done?

Preservation of universe can be of two types— first, the narrow concept of preserving and protecting our planet, Earth, by humans and animals etc. to keep the ecological and environmental balance, and second, the broader concept, to preserve the universe and its inhabitants, from severe and catastrophic disasters / misadventures, caused by some humans or demons for their vested interests. Here, we would be considering only the second type. It means that God sovereignly, by a continuous agency, maintains in existence all the things which he has created, together with all their properties and powers. It is something like 'Providence' which means continuous activity of God, whereby, he makes all the events of the physical, mental and moral realm work for his purpose and for the creation he has already made. Evils, destructive forces may enter the universe, but God will not allow the evils and destructive forces to thwart God's original purpose and may destroy the evils etc.

Answer to the question 'Who' is very clear and that is the Brahman, in the form of Lord Vishnu. As to 'why' the preservation is needed, few of the answers may be as follows-

i- To restore the universe or any part of that, after catastrophic disaster / misadventure or annihilation of humankind or other lives done or attempted by some human or demons; i.e. to destroy evil and restore justice in the world.

ii- He is the divine arbitrator. He protects justice and moral order by mediating disagreements, whether they involve humans or gods.

iii- He is a personification we might call on when seeking protection, patience, salvation, deliverance.

Before discussing the 3rd question, "How", we would discuss a bit about 'lifecycle management' and 'terotechnology' of any corporate entity, which has reasonable parallelism with the preservation of universe.

5.2.1   Lord Vishnu's Model of corporate preservation

Peace loving Lord Vishnu plays the role of preserver or sustainer and he does that with his steadfast principles of order, righteousness and truth. In any corporate entity, company's core values need to be preserved. Values and practices that promote high performance and integrity are to be promoted and an excellent corporate culture is to be attained through hiring, training and promoting people who endorse the corporate values. In the same way, Lord Vishnu principle comes into being and institutionalization must take place. As discussed later in Sec.5.10, Lord Vishnu's reclining (Anantasana) pose indicates that the leaders in any corporation should keep calm and be patient in the face of fear and worries that the poisonous snake depicts and let not fear overpower them and disturb their peace. Like Vishnu continues to eliminate bad elements (demons or otherwise) to protect/preserve good people and culture, in corporations also bad practices should be eliminated so that new values and practices can be put into place and be nurtured. Again, for advanced care and preservation, Lord Vishnu continues to manifest on the earth in the form of a great soul for a specific purpose, generally as a seer, a guru , a ruler, or an artist, called partial manifestation or 'ansh-avatar' / 'minor avatars' (Sec.5.8). In the same way, corporate entity has to continuously improve knowledge, techniques, management and integration etc. by various methods like Kaizen, Six Sigma, Total Quality Control, Life Cycle Management (LCM) and Terotechnology etc., the last two of which will be discussed in next two sections. Again, like in a corporate entity, for intensive care, major overhauls & turnarounds are adopted, Lord Vishnu does the intensive care of universe by his major avatars.

Few of the salient points for preservation are as follows-

1- Follow-up / implement the strategic and long-range planning, (one to five years) for goals of the organization, normally given at planning stage and arrange necessary resources.
2- Do tactical planning (normally less than two years), based on strategic planning.
3- Do operational planning, creating specific standards, methods, policies and procedures that are used in specific areas of the organization.
4- Do contingency planning, identifying alternative courses of actions for very unusual crisis situations.

5.3   Life-Cycle Approach (LCA / LCM)

We have discussed life-cycle approach for universe and corporation briefly in chapters 2 & 3. Here we would discuss in some more detail. We used the bathtub curve approach, as the curve looks like a bathtub. Other names for the lifecycle approach are 'womb to tomb approach' or 'cradle to grave approach'.

Life Cycle Approach (LCA) or Life-cycle Management (LCM) is a business management approach that can be used by all types of business (and other organizations / corporations) in order to improve their sustainability and performance. It is about making life cycle thinking and product sustainability operational for businesses that are aiming for continuous improvement. It is a technique to assess environmental impacts associated with all the stages of a product's life from raw material extraction through materials processing, manufacture, distribution, use, repair and maintenance, and disposal or recycling. Designers use this process to help analyze their products. It can help avoid a narrow outlook on environmental concerns by preparing an inventory of relevant energy and material inputs and environmental effects, analyzing their potential impacts and interpreting the results to make more informed decisions.

LCM is of two types--- Plant Lifecycle Management and Product Lifecycle Management. With reference to the governance of universe, Plant Lifecycle Management is more applicable, and we would consider that. Plant lifecycle management is the process of managing an industrial facility's data and information throughout its lifetime. It differs from product lifecycle management by its primary focus on the integration of logical, physical and technical plant data in a combined plant model. Fig. 5.2 shows a general model or flow diagram of LCA or LCM. It has following seven stages. The factors affecting first five stages have already been discussed in Sec.4.9. The last two stages will be given more emphasis here.

1- Specification
2- Design & development
3- Manufacturing, construction and acquisition, both onsite and offsite
4- Erection and installation
5- Testing, commissioning & handing over to operating & maintenance personnel, with necessary onsite training,
6- Operation & Maintenance- Operating personnel have to guard against bad operating practices, bad inputs, bad inspection / monitoring gadgets, batch vis-à-vis continuous production and lapse in quality control etc. Maintenance personnel should guard against bad maintenance practices, any design fault, online and offline equipment condition monitoring gadgets. Maintenance should continue to take necessary refurbishing for life extension of plant and equipment.
7- Replacement or Disposal- Exploring reasons like worn-out beyond repairs, obsolescence (spares / raw materials or product), uneconomic (better and cheaper alternatives come-up), excess pollution and environment not friendly etc. to help decide replacement or disposal. This stage also involves decommissioning safely prior to disposal

and also land rehabilitation, i.e. returning the land in a given area to some degree of its former state, after some process (industry, natural disasters, etc.) has resulted in its damage.

Fig.5.2 shows how the activities and focus moves from specification to design, manufacture, install, commission, operate / maintain and to replace or dispose and each stage being monitored from top. Feedback is very important at every stage between concerned agencies for immediate correction of any deviation / fault in order to achieve optimum result at optimum cost. In the figure, few essential feedbacks are shown by broken lines.

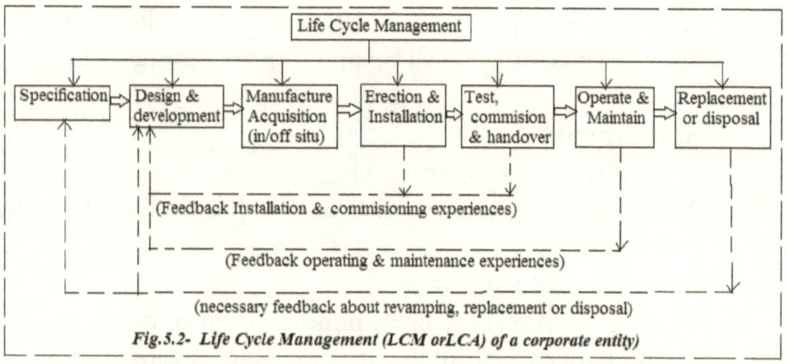

Fig.5.2- Life Cycle Management (LCM orLCA) of a corporate entity)

5.4   Preservation vis-à-vis Terotechnology

Terotechnology is yet another concept like 'lifecycle approach' or 'lifecycle management' but laying more emphasis on maintenance and preservation of the establishment or corporate entity. Terotechnology is the maintenance of assets in optimal manner. It is the combination of management, financial, engineering, and other practices applied to physical assets such as plant, machinery, equipment, buildings and structures in pursuit of economic life cycle costs. It also accounts for the processes of installation, commissioning, operation, maintenance, modification and replacement or disposal. The goals of this multidisciplinary approach are to reduce the different costs incurred at the various stages of an asset's life and to develop methods that will help extend its life span. Terotechnology is more of a management technique or a subsystem of organizational practices than strictly a technology.

Though the goal of both, LCM and Terotechnology, is practically same, their approach and emphasis are little different. The minor difference between the two are as follows-

- For LCM / LCA, the main emphasis is on optimizing life cycle cost (LCC), i.e. total cost throughout its life, including planning, design, manufacture, operation, maintenance, support cost and other costs directly attributable to owning and using the asset (all the initial costs, operating costs and disposal costs). But for terotechnology, the main emphasis is optimum preservation and of 'caring-for' plant and equipment in order to pursue economic life cycle cost. To some extent, it has to recognize the difficulties of problems of estimation, forecasting and inflation etc.

- LCM / LCA is a broader concept and can be applied to all types of organizations, including government organizations, transport and distribution organizations, but Terotechnology is, generally, preferred for manufacturing and process industries.

Some experts have coined the term "Terotechnological Life Cycle" which is a cyclic process during which a plant is prepared for operational use, put into use and maintained so that it remains in an operational condition and is finally removed from use at the end of its life. However, it is nothing more than what have been discussed earlier. As such, the model of flow diagram for terotechnology or 'Terotechnological Life Cycle' will be almost similar to Fig.5.2.

Few of the benefits of Terotechnology are as followings-
i-   Better maintenance and higher reliability of plants, equipment and systems.

ii-   Lower cost of maintenance and repair.
iii-   Lesser breakdowns / outages.
iv-   Higher quality and better efficiency of operations and processes.
v-   Better image of the corporate entity amongst customers and suppliers.
vi-   Better communication between producer, customers, suppliers, vendors and other.

5.4.1   Levels of tribological cares / preservations

As terotechnology is 'caring-for' or preservation of plant and equipment in order to pursue economic life cycle cost, its care and preservation activities can, broadly, include following three stages-

1- General Care / preservation- These include simple practices, that could be applied in almost all organizations/industries at each phase of an asset's 'terotechnological life-cycle'. These also encompass those practices which would require a reasonable commitment of resources in order to apply terotechnological practices during an asset's lifecycle.

2- Advanced Care / preservation- The activities / practices, adopted at this level, could be associated with a considerable degree of development in the application of terotechnology. Such practices could be expected to provide a comprehensive life-cycle management system for an organization's physical assets. To operate at this level-of-care / preservation, it would require a higher commitment of resources over and above those employed at the 'general care level'.

3- Intensive Care / preservation- Cares / activities of this stage calls for very high degree of concentrated, unremitting commitment of resources and asset's life and provides a system of detailed monitoring and observation of plant performance with subsequent intensive analysis and treatment. This could be considered as the level at which an organization has developed a complete terotechnologically based physical asset life-cycle management system.

Activities / practices of all the three stages mentioned above can, again, be classified in two categories---

- Monitoring Cares- related to monitoring and control of various jobs / activities.
- Intensity of Cares- related to intensity and volume of preservation / repair jobs.

Table T-5.1 gives list of essential items/cares of all the three levels in both the categories.

Table T-5.1- Levels & categories of Tribological cares/preservations

Type of are Level of Care	Monitoring Care	Intensity of Care
General Care & Preservation,	Maintenance checklists & Inspection schedules, job-cards, Operator's checklists & inspection Schedules, job-cards, Lubrication schedules, Time-based Preventive Maintenance, Spare parts Codification & catalogs, Budgets, etc.	Reactive Maintenance (Breakdowns & mini Repairs), Opportunistic maintenance, Time-based Maintenance
Advanced Care & Preservation	Standard operating practices / manuals, Standard Maintenance procedures / Manuals & work-measurement methods, Standard costing, Performance monitoring indicators, Machine condition monitoring indicators, (online & offline monitoring), Predictive	Major planned condition- based maintenance, Annual Overhauls, Statutory Overhauls

	maintenance & condition Based maintenance schedules, Data management, In-company data feedback, etc.	
Intensive Care & Preservation	Failure mode & criticality analysis & Risk-analysis, Continuous online monitoring & Feedback for machines, processes & products, Proactive maintenance, Total Productive maintenance & Lean maintenance, & Web-based maintenance schedules, Out-company data feedback, Trade-off analysis & optimization, etc.	Maintenance Turnaround & Outage management, Revamping & Refurbishing

In-company data feedback should ensure that relevant information on plant design, installation, performance and cost characteristics are available to all functional groups, in the company, with responsibility for those characteristics. Out-company data feedback is a system of information feedback to suppliers, contractors, equipment designers, and other external organizations. This can also include useful feedback between different companies of the same corporation, existing at different locations and working on Web-based system. Trade-off analysis & optimization take the form of simulating the operating, reliability, maintainability and cost characteristics, performing balancing studies and optimization techniques in order to develop an optimum terotechnologically based preservation and up-keep policy. Proactive maintenance is a maintenance strategy that works to correct the root causes of failure and avoid breakdowns caused by unrevealed equipment conditions. The purpose of proactive maintenance is to see machine failures as something that can be anticipated and eliminated before they develop. Adopting proactive maintenance program helps organizations find hidden inefficiencies, by taking use of various monitoring gadgets. 'Maintenance turnaround' is as the planned outage of the shop / plant to completely overhaul equipment and plant so that it will become almost new and will have a full operating life. 'Outage management system' is a computer system used by operators of electric distribution systems to assist in restoration of power. It calls for prediction of location of equipment, prioritization, calculations and management.

Other terms, mentioned in the table, are more common. We would not go in details of those. The purpose of this section (Sec.5.4 & Sec.5.4.1) is to show that how Lord Vishnu preserves the universe with somewhat similar methods, which would be discussed in subsequent paras.

5.5   Vishnu's Preservation of universe through Avatars

Coming back to preservation of universe, Bhagavad Gita says that whenever evil gains ascendance, Lord Vishnu incarnates on earth to restore dharma, punish the evil and protect the weak and the righteous. He uses both force and guile to ensure the stability of the universe. He makes the adjustments for the proper administration of the cosmic creation. In-course of preservation, he also gives everyone the ability to act and function through the power of the Brahman in His form as the Super-soul. He provides the life force and consciousness to everyone, and, thus, maintains the creation. But, unlike Lord Brahma, Lord Vishnu doesn't directly produce sons and daughters to help Him in preservation jobs, but he himself takes avatars (incarnates) in the different form of different beings, thru different means for different purposes or different types of preservation jobs, and, sometimes, after the required job is done, that incarnation dies and dissolves back in Lord Vishnu. Of-course, his incarnations have their sons and daughters etc., but they may or may not be much connected to preservation of universe.

Vishnu has always been associated with economic activities. As Krishna, as cowherd, he is linked to animal husbandry, while his elder brother, Balarama, holds a plough and is linked to agriculture. As Ram, he is considered fair and just, alluding to proper distribution of wealth. Vishnu is linked to an ocean of milk, to butter, to rivers, to woods, to farmlands and pasturelands. He wears silk fabric, assuming the existence of farmers, spinners, weavers, dyers and washers. He wears gold ornaments, assuming the existence of miners, smelters, smiths and jewelers. Vishnu is shown enjoying good life and, thru this, he shows that everyone should enjoy good life. He preserves the universe thru good governance, wealth distribution and Dharma.

Though we are not certain about the authenticity of the list of incarnations or the events associated with many of the incarnations, the idea of incarnation itself is a reasonable and logically acceptable. God chooses different ways to restore order and balance in the universe. Vishnu as Maha-Vishnu (Brahman) can be said to have different types of avatars, mainly as mentioned below. Many of the Avatars may come in more than one type.

1- Purusha Avatars- Karanodakashayi Vishnu or Maha-Vishnu (Sankarsana), the cause of all causes, i.e. Vishnu lying on the causal ocean and creator of "Mahat-Tattva"; Garbhodakashayi Vishnu (Pradyumna), i.e. Vishnu lying on Sheshanag in the universal ocean and Purusha immanent in Brahma Eggs; Kshirodakashayi Vishnu (Aniruddha), i.e. Vishnu lying on the milk ocean and Paramatma dwelling in each creature. Normally the 3rd Vishnu (Kshirodakashayi) is referred as part of Trinity and maintainer of universe.

2- Lila avatars (pastime incarnations), such as 4-Kumaras, Narada, Nar-Narayan, Duttatreya, Pruthu, Vyasa etc.

3- Manvantara Avatars- Each of the 14 manvantaras have one incarnation of Vishnu. For our present manvantara, the avatar is Vamana.

4- Yuga Avatars- Each of the Yugas have avatars. Krishna was the avatar of last Dvapara Yuga.

5- Avesha Avatars (Empowerment incarnation)- e.g. 4-Kumaras (empowered with knowledge), Narada (empowered with devotional service), King Prithu, empowered with power to maintain living beings etc.

6- Vibhava form (Avatar)- Various manifestations, including the popular 10 Avatar, from time to time, to protect the virtuous, punish evil-doers and re-establish righteousness.

7- Antaryami form ('Dwelling within' or 'Suksma Vasudeva' form) in which Vishnu exists within the souls of all living beings and in every substance.

However, for the sake of preservation of universe, most of the Vishnu's incarnations can broadly be classified into following categories, which logically appears in line with the three terotechnological levels of cares mentioned in Sec.5.4.1.

a- Incorporeal Avatars, for general care & preservation,
b- Minor Avatars (Ansh Avatars), for advanced cares & preservations,
c- Mega Avatars (Full Avatars), for intensive cares & preservation.
d- A fourth category may be Non-Avatar prophets, inventors, and saints of revelations who were able to open specific channels of communication with God or whom God would choose to speak. This may include Patanjali, Agastya, Sai Baba, Shankaracharya, Swaminarayana and likes. However, we would not discuss much about this category as this category tends to include few fake ones.

We would discuss the above three categories of avatars further in this chapter. Fig.5.3 shows the organization chart of Vishnu, indicating the three care level categories.

Lord Vishnu gets the general care and preservation of universe done thru his incorporeal Avatars. It means Lord Vishnu has incarnated somewhere else, either created by Brahma or given birth by Aditi or incorporeally in any other way and help preservation of Earth / universe in general way. Truly speaking, all the manifestations of Brahman as various gods, goddesses and deities in various worlds are but His incarnations only and can be included in this category. Thru this route, Vishnu sets up the universal demigods / deities and the kings/ controllers of different planets (esp. 9 grahas) to continue overseeing the maintenance of the universe. All the 33 types of deities / demigods (12 Adityas + 11 Rudras + 8 Vasus + 2 others) and other deities produced by these 33 deities or otherwise, serve, in some way or other, for preservation of universe. Because of the benediction and power given by Lord Vishnu to the demigods, they can provide the living beings with required necessities. As part of the preservation of the worlds and Dharma, they also perform many duties such as guiding the souls who are on their way to ancestral heaven or the immortal heaven, making things auspicious, preventing natural calamities, removing misfortune and protecting people from their enemies. However, they are created in such a way that they cannot exist without the help of humans. They exist both in the macrocosm of the universe and the microcosm of a living being. Despite their immense powers and supernatural abilities, they have to depend upon humans for their nourishment. Humans have the obligation to perform daily sacrifices and respects / worship to nourish the gods. In this way, there can be proper cooperation between human, nature and God so that everyone can be peaceful and content with the facilities for living in this world.

There are very many gods and goddesses in this category who handle different divisions providing different types of general cares, few of which are given in Table T-5.1. The table gives 23 deities, including 7 of the 9 Grahas.

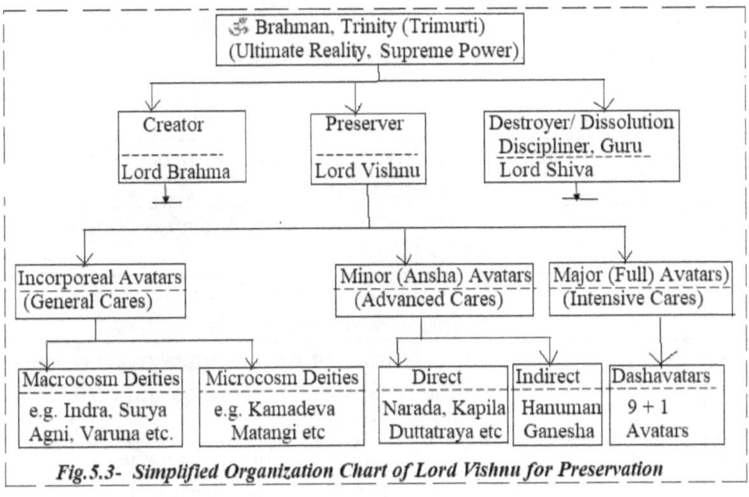

Fig.5.3- *Simplified Organization Chart of Lord Vishnu for Preservation*

Table T-5.2- Incorporeal avatars of Vishnu for general care/preservation

#	Name of Devas / Devi	Functions / Divisions of responsibility
1	Indra (also called Sakra); Parjanya	King of Devas; also, I/c of division of thunder, storms & rains Management, including pouring sufficient rain
2	Agni (Anala)	I/c division of fire resources & lighting; also blesses via Homa (sacrifice ritual fire), aarti & lamp etc.
3	Annapurna Devi (Annada)	I/c division of food and nourishment, kitchen & cookery
4	Brihaspati (Deva-Guru)	I/c division of teaching and Guru of knowledge & character development, piety and religion
5	Budha (Mercury)	I/c division of speech, logic, intellect, discrimination
6	Chandra (Soma); Moon God	I/c division of lighting during night & inspiration for poetry and beauty; also, Lord of plants, tidal waves & intoxicating drinks.
7	Chitragupta	I/c division of archive and record-keeping
8	Dhat (Dhatri)	I/c division of health, magic / tantra and domestic tranquility.
9	Kamadeva	I/c of division of human love, desire and inciting power,

10	Kartikeya (Murugan, Skanda, Subrahmanya)	I/c division of war & defense; also, commander of devas.
11	Kubera (Bhaga)	I/c division of wealth & prosperity management
12	Mangala	Deity of war, energy & aggression, like Kartikeya,
13	Matangi	I/c division of super-natural powers, tantras & spoken words.
14	Pushan	I/c division of travels, tours (road & other modes) & social gatherings and cattle transport/ feeding
15	Shani	I/c division of justice & benefits / punishments depending on individual's Karma
16	Shashthi	I/c division of reproduction, children & also vegetation
17	Shitala (Sheetala)	I/c division of cures for poxes, sores, ghouls, pustules and diseases.
18	Shukracharya	I/c division of teaching & knowledge of demons
19	Surya (Sun, Bhanu, Vivasvat, Savitar)	I/c division of light, warmth and whole solar energy system / management
20	Varuna	I/c of division of river, ocean & its creatures management
21	Vayu (Anila)	I/c wind power and its resources,
22	Vishvakarma (Tvastr)	Chief architect & I/c of artisans, architects, engineers & fashioners,
23	Yama	I/c division of Dharma (moral ethics), death and justice.

All the incorporeal avatars can, again, be classified in two categories---

    a- Macrocosm deities- Personification of the natural phenomena like Indra – god of rain, Vayu – god of wind, Agni – god of fire, Varuna – god of the sea, Yama – god of death etc.

b- Microcosm deities- —Personification of psychological forces, such as Kamadeva (desire).

Again, just as in any corporate entity, different divisional in-charges are only administrative posts, not individuals, we can believe that these Devas / incorporeal avatars are administrative posts and not individuals, so every one of us can aspire to become an administrative Deva. The Devas / deities are the forces of "light" the integrating powers of the Cosmos.

5.6.1   Parallelism with other mythologies

Hinduism is not the only religion where different deities / gods are depicted with different function. Table T-5.3 gives corresponding deities from few other religions / mythologies for few of the functions. The table is just illustrative and includes only few mythologies. This table has been given only with the intention to prove that the Almighty God is one and only one and different mythologies depict the preservation of universe by that God in somewhat similar ways with cosmetic and situational changes.

Table T-5.3- Parallelism of deities of different mythologies

Mythology / Deities	Hinduism	Persian	Greek	Chinese	Norse	Egypt
Earth deity	Bhu Devi	Zam-Armatay	Gaia	Tudigong	Jord	Geb
Love deity	Kamadeva	Anahita	Aphrodite, Erotes	Yue-Lao	Freyja	Hathor
Lunar Deity	Chandra	Mah	Selene	Chang Xi	Mani	Iah
Psychopomps	Yamaraja	Daena	Charon	Ox-head & Horse-face	Valkyries	Anubis
Solar Deity	Surya / Mitra	Mithra	Helios/ Apollo	Xihi	Sunna	Ra / Atum
War deity	Kartikeya / Mangal	Rostam	Ares	Chiyou	Tyr, Odin	Sekhmet Horus
Water Deity	Varuna	Tiamat	Poseidon	Mazu	Ran	Tefnut
Wind Deity	Vayu	Vayu-Vata,	Aeolus	Fei Lian,	Njord	Amun, Shu
Wisdom & Learning	Saraswati Ganesha Brihaspati	Anahita	Athena Metis	Wenchang-Wang	Kvasir, Odin Allfather	Thoth

5.7   Advanced Cares / Preservation

Lord Vishnu gets the advanced care and preservation of universe thru his minor Avatars. It means only an aspect (ansha) of him manifests on the earth in the form of a great soul for a specific purpose, generally as a seer, a guru , a ruler, or an artist, and, as such, it is called partial manifestation or 'ansha-avatar'. It may be for limited period and after performing the desired task, the avatar vanishes and merges with Vishnu, or may be for longer period for the desired task. Again, ansha-avatars may be of two types- 'Direct', i.e. ansha-avatar of Vishnu and 'Indirect', i.e. minor incarnation or sons/daughters of other Gods but helping Lord Vishnu for advanced care/preservation of Universe. There may be many direct ansha-avatars of Vishnu, out of which few are given in Table T-5.4.

Table T-5.4- Ansha (minor) avatars of Vishnu for advanced care/preservation

#	Avatar	Brief Descriptions
1	4 Kumaras (Sanakadika Rishis)	'Manasputras' of Lord Brahma. Throughout their life, they maintained celibacy; and engaged themselves in the performance of tremendous penance. They preached the values and importance of penance, Celibacy, Vedas & transcendental knowledge.
2	Narada	Narada, a 'Devarishi' among sages, portrays that the devotion is the best mean of getting liberated from all the bondages of 'Karma's'. He also said that a devotee of Lord Vishnu is the supreme among the devotees. He is known for travelling and informing / broadcasting.
3	Nara-Narayana	Nara Narayana were twin sage brothers, born to Yama Deva, did severe penance for welfare of human and also killed the demon called Sahasrakavacha (Demon with a thousand armors). Nara Narayana, later, reincarnated as Arjuna and Lord Krishna and Sahasrakavacha as Karna.

4	Kapila	The objective of incarnation of Kapila (as son of Rishi Kardama) was to compile all the divine knowledge that had been destroyed. He was the profounder of Sankhya Shastra (rationalism) which helped the Brahmins, who had forgotten their duties, to rectify their mistakes. He is identified as a recluse associated with Yogic adepts (siddha*s*).
5	Dattatraya	Born to Anasuya & sage Atri, Dattatraya was the one who had given Spiritual Knowledge to King Alarka and Prahlada. He believed that in the world, a man can learn from each and everything, so he accepted twenty-four objects like water, bird, air, an unmarried girl, and even a prostitute etc. as his gurus. He taught the system of mystic yoga and some tantras. Sometimes he is depicted with 3 heads and 6 arms, indicating that he was the incarnation of Trimurti.
6	Yajna	Yajna or Yajneshwara (Lord of Yajna, i.e. ritual sacrifice) was son of Prajapati Ruci and Akuti. He was king of heaven (like Indra) in Svayambhuva Manu era. The main thrust of his teaching was based on the values of helpfulness and protecting each other during the time of crisis.
7	Rishabha,	Rishabha, meaning morality, was one of the hundred sons of Nabhi and his wife Meru. He attained that state of Paramhansa (an ascetic of highest order who has controlled his anger) which is an uphill task. He was given the title of 'Jina' which means a ' a knower'.
8	Prithu	Prithu, the first man to be crowned as a king, was the son of Vena, born of his thigh. The earth had concealed all the vegetation's within her and as a result the whole land had become barren. To protect the humanity, Lord Vishnu took this incarnation by milking the cow (earth). The earth has remained full of vegetation's after that.
9	Dhanwantari	He is a solar divinity embodied as the physician of the Gods. He was evolved from

		the Samudra Manthan carrying in his hands the pot containing amrita (nectar of immorality). He was the profounder of medicinal science.
10	Mohini	During Samudra Manthan, Lord Vishnu took the form of an exceedingly beautiful woman, Mohini to prevent the demons from consuming the amrita. After distributing the drink to the Devas, Mohini flew away with it. Vishnu took yet another form of Mohini when demon Bhasmasura, after getting the boon from Lord Shiva, wanted to burn Shiva. Mohini, during dance, tricked Bhasmasura to put his hand on his head and thus burn himself.
11	Hayagreeva/ Hayashirsha	Once demons Madhu and Kaitabha stole the Vedas while Lord Brahma was asleep, and dove into the ocean with Vedas. Vishnu took this horse-headed incarnation with four hands and human body, went at the bottom of ocean, killed the demons and retrieved the Vedas. As such, he is, also, worshipped as the god of knowledge and wisdom.
12	Vyas (Ved-Vyas)	Son of Satyavati & sage Parashar, Vyas is the compiler of Vedas. He made the division of Veda and made extension of its branches. He also wrote eighteen Mahapuranas and the Mahabharata. His disciples were Sumanta, Jaimini, Paila etc.
13	Buddha	Bhagvata Purana says that when the demons planned to perform Yagya so that they could regain power and authority over devas, Vishnu took Buddha avatar (born as Siddhartha Gautama) to dissuade the demons from performing Yagya as it involves violence and animal sacrifice. Buddha went on to start Buddhism. Buddha's teaching takes care of the widespread devolution of morality and wisdom that is inevitable in the Kali Yuga.

The indirect category of Ansha-avatars of Vishnu may include Hanuman, Ganesha, Garuda and Adishesha etc. They were born

/ created thru other Gods but helped Vishnu's incarnations in preserving the universe. Hanuman, an incarnation of Shiva, born to Anjani, was the chief help of Lords Rama. He is shown as cheerful (prasannanjaneya), ferocious (Veeranjaneya), meditating (dhayananjaneya) or in a mood of devotion (bhaktanjaneya). Garuda eagle is the Vehicle of Vishnu. Empowered with the courage and speed to spread the knowledge of the Vedas, Garuda is an assurance of fearlessness at the time of calamity. Ganesha is well known to all Hindus and many non-Hindus. He is the son of Lord Shiva but helped Vishnu in many ways to preserve the universe. He is known as remover of obstacles. He is also known as first worshipped God. Symbolically, Adishesha represents the materiality of creation. Since Vishnu rests upon him before, during and after creation, he is considered indestructible.

5.8   Intensive Cares / Preservation

Lord Vishnu gets the intensive care and preservation of universe done thru his major (full) Avatars. It means Lord Vishnu descends directly, either in human form or in any other form, with all his powers and, as such, these Avatars are called full manifestation of 'purna-avatar'. He assumes this form only when an evil of gigantic dimensions rises its head and start fomenting trouble everywhere.

T-5.5 - 10 Major Avatars of Vishnu for Intensive care of Universe

# A	# B	Avatar	Yuga	Brief Descriptions
1	2	Matsya (Fish), half fish, half man	Satya	When the world was on the brink of cosmic deluge, caused by Demon 'Maya', with heavy rain and no land left to stay, Vishnu, in the form of great fish, asked the then Manu (King Satyavrat) to make a big boat and load with one species of all lives & Vedas and, then, the

				fish carried the boat to safe mountain to start anew.
2	3	Kurma (Tortoise)	Satya	Once, in order to get Amrita (Nectar of Immortality), Devas & Asuras started churning the ocean (Samundra Manthan), using serpent Vasuki as rope and Mount Mandara as churning staff. But, with its sheer weight, Mount Mandara started sinking & going towards netherworld. Then Lord Vishnu, in the form of a tortoise, supported the Mount Mandara on Himself & thus saved the world and Samundra Manthan was continued.
3	1	Varaha (Boar)	Satya	This has earlier been mentioned in Sec. 4.7.2. When the demon Hiranyaksha tormented the earth (personified as the goddess Bhudevi) and sank the Earth into the Rasaatal (lower portion of Cosmic Ocean), Vishnu, in the form of a boar, descended into the depths of the oceans, slew the demon and retrieved the Earth from the ocean, lifting her on his tusks, and restored Bhudevi to her place in the universe.
4	4	Narasimha (Half Lion, Half Man)	Satya	The demon Hiranyakashipu, the elder brother of Hiranyaksha, was granted a boon from Brahma that he could not be killed by man or animal, inside or outside a room, during day or night, neither on ground nor in air, and nor with any weapon. He persecuted everyone for their religious beliefs including his son,

					Prahlada, who was a Vishnu follower. Vishnu descended with the body of a man and head and claws of a lion. He disemboweled Hiranyakashipu at the courtyard threshold of his house, at dusk, with his claws, while he lay the demon on his thighs. Narasimha thus destroyed the evil demon and brought an end to the persecution of human beings.
5	5	Vamana (Dwarf)		Treta	Asura King Bali, 4th descendant of Hiranyakashipu, had acquired disproportionate power over the universe and conquered entire three worlds and Indra & other devas lost their abode and heaven. However, he was a noble demon king and gave gift at ceremonies to consolidate his power. To help Devas regain their heaven, Vishnu appeared at that ceremony as a dwarf mendicant brahmin called Vamana and asked for land measuring his three steps. When Bali agreed, Vamana grew into a giant of cosmic proportions. In one step he covered the earth, in another the heavens, and for the third, Bali offered his head on which Vamana stepped, sending the demon king to the Pataala (netherworld).
6	6	Parashura ma		Treta	Parashurama, the warrior with the axe, is the first Brahmin-Kshatriya or warrior-saint, with duties between a Brahmin and a Kshatriya. When the

				Kshatriya kings became ruthless and started exploiting their subjects, Lord Vishnu incarnated as Parshurama and annihilated the Kshatriyas kings for seventeen times and consequently donated the earth to the Brahmins and others. As Parasurama is an immortal, he appeared both in the Ramayana era as well as in Mahabharata era.
7	7	Rama	Treta	Lord Rama was the one of the two most popular and first perfect man avatar of Vishnu. He is famous for being honorable and heroic, even giving up his right to rule his kingdom and going into exile because his father asked it of him. With the help of Lakshmana, Hanuman and others, Rama eliminated multiheaded demon Ravana and most other demons who had become severe menace to society. His story, Ramayana is known and revered by all.
8	8	Balarama	Dwapar	Balarama is said to be the elder brother of Krishna. It is believed that he was engaged in many adventures alongside Lord Krishna. His stories always focus on his prodigious strength. In this incarnation Lord Vishnu killed demons Pralambasura, Dhenukasura and Mushtika etc. Balarama is sometimes considered as the Sankarshana form of Vishnu. Scriptures also say that Balarama as an avatar of

				Sheshanaga – the companion of Vishnu.
9	9	Krishna	Dwapar	Krishna is the most famous of all of Vishnu's avatars. He is known for destroying countless evil kings and demons and being a key figure in the Mahabharata and the Battle of Kurukshetra. His gyana and advices to Arjuna at the battlefield became the famous Bhagwat Gita, laying down the foundation of principles to help mankind. He saved Draupadi from public humiliation. He set an example for modern-day spirituality and self-realization. His many stories are well known and revered by all.
10	10	Kalki	Kali	Towards the end of Kali Yuga, when only chaos, evil and persecution prevails and dharma has vanished, Lord Vishnu will appear on horse, blazing like a comet and will end almost entire existence and pave way to start a new Satya Yuga.

NB.1-- #A is the most accepted sequence of the mega 10 Avatars
2-- #B is the sequence as per Bhagavata Purana's Avatars
3-- Some consider the sequence little differently. They consider Krishna as Avatar no. 8 and Lord Buddha as Avatar no.9. They merge Balarama with Krishna Avatar as they both existed at the same time.

In His job as preserver, Lord Vishnu is the savior of everyone, including gods, goddesses and even Lord Shiva. When demon Bhasmasura, after getting the boon from Lord Shiva, wanted to burn Lord Shiva, Lord Vishnu, as Mohini, tricked Bhasmasura to burn himself.

5.8.1   Important lessons from Vishnu

From above, esp. from Krishna Avatar, we learn the following important lessons-

1- Everything happens for a reason-- We shouldn't waste our time lamenting over the past or getting overly anxious about the future.

2- Value Love-- Love everyone (including animals) with a childlike simplicity. Don't expect anything in return, nor held animosity towards them when they didn't give back.

3- Be Non-judgmental-- In God's eyes, everyone or everything is equal. Don't start judging (if good or bad for us) immediately every happening as it happens. This is the main theme of present day's mindfulness movement.

4- Believe in yourself and believe in God-- Each one of us has the ability to tap into unlimited resources of the universe.

5- Be aware of your dharma & purpose of living-- Dharma is the duty to which we are all bound; it's the purpose for living. Being aware of our purpose of living and working towards that, fulfils our life with sense of satisfaction.

6- Nothing really belongs to us-- We came empty-handed and we will go empty -handed. Whatever we got, we got from God. Whatever we gave, we gave to God.

7- Don't be an imposter-- If we are going to preach a spiritual life to others, we should be leading one. Never lie to oneself-- find one's truth and stick to it.

8- Karma is real-- It is somewhat like Newton's law that every action has equal & opposite reaction. Whatever you do will come back to you at some point. Our actions have consequences and will affect our next birth.

9- Surrender to the Almighty and do our duty without expecting return for that. Believe that not everything is under our control. We should learn to 'let go'.

5.9   Organization of Preserver, Lord Vishnu

Lord Vishnu is the preserver, protector, sustainer, and guardian of the earth / universe. As shown in Fig.3.1, Vishnu (along with Goddess Lakshmi), as preserver, has all the resources in abundance. Lakshmi's presence near Vishnu balances his male intellect and spiritual sophistication with female physicality and passion, essential for his performance. His rough organization chart, for preserving the universe has already been shown in Fig. 5.2. Few of his mission and special characteristics are as follows:

1- He is the deity of nourishment (annarasadevata), the one who nurtures all living beings.

2- He is gentle and of merciful nature. He loves His devotees (bhaktavatsal). He rushes to rescue his devotees when he feels necessary, even when he has to take some curse upon himself for that.

3- He is the one who maintains the balance of the universe. Unlike Brahma, he is not attached to the organization. Unlike Shiva, he is not disengaged from it. He creates balance and harmony by necessary amount of creation and necessary amount of destruction also and he is always aware of the 'big picture'. However, Vishnu's cycle of creation, preservation and destruction is in little different ratio, i.e. 3:94:3 and not 9:82:9 for bigger cycle as shown in Fig.5.1. Often Brahma, because of his simplicity and sometime Lord Shiva give few demons boons with immense power and with that the demons start destroying living beings on universe. It is left to

Lord Vishnu to find ways to destroy those demons or their demonic powers.

4- He is the divine arbitrator. He protects justice and moral order by mediating disagreements, whether they involve humans or gods. (Refer Sec.5.2).

5- He is a stable deity. He functions without leaving his seat because he exists everywhere, where-ever the need may be. His abode is in Vishnu's region (Vaikunth-Lok or Vaikuntha-Sagar). He also lives in celestial ocean (Kshirasagar), because his wife, Lakshmi came from the churning of the primordial ocean (Samudra Manthan). Yet his real abode is where his devotees sing his glory.

6- Vishnu can be said as Lord of Sattva Guna (virtue of truth), as Rajas Guna goes to Brahma, who comes out from Vishnu's naval and the Sheshnag snake stands for the vices of fear and darkness or 'Tamas Guna'.

7- Vishnu is made of both automatic and manual forces in equal magnitude and gives us the ability to do two things at the same time.

8- Vishnu is the purifier of life. Vishnu symbolizes water. This is the reason why most Hindus symbolically immerse ash and idols of Durga, Ganesh etc. into water, i.e. in Maha-Vishnu.

In addition to above special characteristics, Lord Vishnu's auspicious qualities are countless. His six most-important "divine glories" are given here below-

a- Omniscience (Gyana), the power to know about all beings simultaneously,
b- Sovereignty (Aishvarya), derived from the word Ishvara, meaning unchallenged rule overall,
c- Energy (Shakti), the capacity to make the impossible possible,

d- Strength (Bala), the capacity to support everything by will, without fatigue,

e- Vigor (Virya), the power to retain immateriality as the Supreme Spirit or Being, despite being the material cause of variable creations,

f- Splendor (Tejas), self-sufficiency and the capacity to overpower everything by spiritual brilliance.

5.9.1   Iconography of Preserver

Vishnu, often, symbolizes the universe with his left eye representing night, his right eye representing day, clouds emerging from his hair and the sun emanating from his mouth. From his nose comes the breath of life, which if properly directed can produce enlightenment.

Lord Vishnu is, mostly, depicted in two poses-- reclining (Anantasana) pose or standing (on lotus or otherwise) pose. Sometimes, he is also depicted in 3rd pose (riding on Garuda or sitting on lotus or otherwise). Anantasana pose depicts as reclining on Sheshanaga-- a coiled, many-headed snake floating on cosmic waters (Kshira Sagar, i.e. ocean of milk) that represent the peaceful universe. This pose symbolizes the calm and patience needed to face our fears and worries, represented here by the poisonous snake. Sheshanaga is said to be expansion of Lord Balarama. The message here is that you should not let fear overpower you and disturb your peace. This pose also indicates that he is present in the entire universe and expands into everything. Symbolically, the ocean stands for bliss and consciousness, snake stands for time, desire and illusion and Goddess Lakshmi stands for the material things and power of the creation.

Though Anantasana pose gives better mythological view, his iconography can, better, be illustrated in standing pose, as given herewith.

1- His sky-blue color symbolizes the sky, formless and infinite.

2- He has four arms-- a pair at the front of his body in lieu
    of his physical presence in the material world, and two at
    the back symbolizing his existence in the spiritual realm.
    His one hand holds a lotus, representing purity, beauty
    and spiritual liberation. Second hand holds a conch shell,
    standing for the sound Aum, said to be the vibration of
    primordial creation, and pervading all spaces. The conch
    shell, named Panchajanya, also represents five elements
    (Panchabhoota). Third hand holds a mace (named
    Kaumodaki), for strength and power for the destruction
    of evil. Few say that the mace is Kali, power of time. It
    destroys all that opposes it. Fourth hand holds a chakra
    (Sudarshan Chakra), emblematic of the mind,
    intelligence, and the end of self-delusion. It also
    represents destruction of ego and, also, destruction of
    evil in any other form. When used as a weapon, it has the
    ability to return to the hand of the person who throws it,
    a quality of the boomerang.

3- It is said that Vishnu's eye is at the Southern Celestial
    Pole from where he watches the cosmos.

4- A crown adorns his head. The crown symbolizes his
    supreme authority. This crown sometimes includes a
    peacock feather, borrowing from his Krishna-avatar.

5- The Shreevatsa mark is on his chest, symbolizing his
    consort Lakshmi.

6- He wears the auspicious "Kaustubha" jewel around his
    neck and a garland of flowers (Vanamala). Lakshmi
    dwells in this jewel, on Vishnu's chest.

7- He wears two earrings: The earrings represent inherent
    opposites in creation — knowledge and ignorance,
    happiness and unhappiness; pleasure and pain.

We have over 1000 names of Lord Vishnu (Vishnu-Sahasranamam), a few are Narayana (which means the shelter, resting place or ultimate goal of all living entities), Hari (one who removes the darkness of illusion), Govinda (One who is attainable by Vedic chanting, Protector of cows), Jagannatha (Juggernaut—owner / Ruler of the world / universe), Janardana (one who is worshiped for Wealth), Madhava (Husband, i.e. Dhava of Lakshmi Maa), Satyanarayana (combination of satya and Narayana meaning 'protector of truth'), Trivikrama (who measured the entire universe in three footsteps in Vamana avatar), Vasudeva (One who resides in all living beings and in turn all living beings reside in him) etc.

Figures / sketches of Lord Vishnu and Lord Shiva will not be given in this book for two reasons—first that there are very many forms of these Gods and second that they are so much in heart and mind of all Hindus and many non-Hindus that giving any sketch will be superfluous.

5.9.2   Direct Relatives

Vishnu is an extraordinary deity and has no limited concept of "family"; rather entire universe is his family. Though few of the Vishnu avatars have their own sons and daughters, the direct relatives of Lord Vishnu are Goddess Lakshmi as wife, Lords Brahma and Shiva as brothers and Parvati, Sarasvati & Ganga as sisters-in-laws. Few say that he, as Lord Vishnu, is beyond any sexual desire and doesn't need procreation and as such has no direct son or daughter. Few others say Padma is daughter, Kama is son, and Rati as daughter-in-law. Some say that Goddess Lakshmi has 18 children. We would not go in further details as Lord Vishnu doesn't necessarily need them for preservation of universe.

~~~~~~~~~~~~~~~~~~~~~~~~~
~~~~~~~~~~~~~~~~~~~~~~~~~

6   Dissolution aspects of Universe and Corporations

(I am proud to belong to a religion which has taught the world both tolerance and universal acceptance. We believe not only in universal tolerance, but we accept all religions as true --- Swami Vivekananda)

Shiva is not just the god of destruction/dissolution, shown as dwelling on the Himalayas or the cremation ground. He is the embodiment of renunciation and destruction of all evil. He is the personification of contemplation and divine consciousness.

6.1   Panchanana (5- Aspects) of Shiva as per Shaivism

The aspects of Shiva can be approached from many perspectives. We have, mostly, considered Shiva as one face / form of Brahman, the supreme power, to do function of destruction / dissolution. But, for many Shaivites, Shiva is the Brahman, the Supreme Power and he takes 5 forms to perform 5 different functions. The following five functions of Shiva are responsible for our existence, continuation, transformation, purification and liberation.

1- Creation (Srishti)- He creates all the worlds and beings, manifesting himself as the individual souls or pure consciousness in the bodies of everyone and in the materiality of all existence.

2- Preservation (Sthithi)- Shiva is also responsible for the continuation of all the worlds and beings. In the body he is the supporting power of breath (prana) and the digestive power of fire (Jatharagni). He is the source of all food and water for gods and living beings.

3- Concealment (Tirobhava)- Shiva, as concealer, casts the net of delusion (maya) upon the whole creation and keeps the living beings deluded, so that the order and regularity of the worlds are not disturbed. Because of his deluding power (maya-shakti), living beings cannot perceive him or realize their own essential nature, which remains suppressed or hidden behind a veil of contaminations.

4- Revelation (Anugraha)- Shiva, as revealer of truth, source of knowledge, and grace, is responsible for the liberation of living beings. None can achieve liberation without his grace. Though good karma is important, the grace of Shiva is even more important to achieve liberation, thru the path of knowledge.

5- Destruction (Samhara)- Shiva, at the end of each cycle of creation, withdraws all worlds and beings into himself and goes into a temporary restful mode. As lord of destruction, he is also responsible for the renewal of life and rebirth of beings.

To execute these five functions, Shiva takes following five forms, which are also depicted as five faced deity (pancha mukha Shiva), in Linga form or otherwise. The different attributes of all these five forms are given in Table T-6.1. We would not go in more details of those.

a- Ishana
b- Tatpurusha
c- Vamadeva
d- Sadyojata
e- Rudra (Aghora)

Table T-6.1, Panchana (5 folds aspects) of Shiva

God \ Attribute	Ishana	Tatpurusha	Vamadeva	Sadyojata	Rudra (Aghora)
Function	Creation, Lord or Total ownership	Preservation	Concealer	Revealer/ Creation	Destroyer
Face direction	Upward	Eastward	North	Westward	South
Element	Ether (space)	Earth	Air	Fire (Agni)	Water
Body Organ	Hands	The Anus	Feet	Mind or Sex organ	Speech
Sense organ	Touch	Smell	Sight	Taste	Hearing
Color	Copper	Golden	Red	White	Black, Dark red
Shakti (Power)	Chit (mind power)	Ananda (Bliss)	Kriya (Action)	Ichha, (will or desire)	Gyana (knowledge)
Kosha (Human Energy body)	Anandamaya (Spiritual body)	Annamaya (Physical body)	Vijnanamaya (Mental body)	Manomaya (Emotional body)	Pranamaya (Etheric body)
Chakra	Vishuddha (Throat+ Ajna & Crown)	Muladhara (Base)	Ānahata (Heart)	Manipura (Solar plexus)	Svadishthana (Sacral)
Few others	Knowledge of Vedas & manifesting power of the mind	Liberating knowledge, the material abundance (Rising sun)	Opposite of Tatpurusha (evening sun), lefthanded. Represents Maya, the grand illusion & feminine strength.	Liberating knowledge, granter of grace, delight & enjoyment.	Non-fearful, battle ready, father of the war gods-- Maruts and Rudras, punitive power of the law (dharma), the power of discrimination

6.1.1 Why Lord Shiva is often worshipped as Lingam

Supreme God, in Yoni-Linga' concept has been discussed in
Sec.1.3.1. There are many stories in Puranas as to why Shiva is
mostly worshipped as Linga or Lingam. One story says that once
Sage Bhrigu went to see Shiva, but Shiva didn't notice Bhrigu's
arrival. Feeling insulted, Bhrigu cursed Shiva to be worshipped
only as lingam on Earth. Another story says that once there was
an argument between Brahma, Vishnu and Shiva as to who is the
greatest. Lord Shiva appeared as a huge pillar of fire that spread
across the universe. He told Brahma and Vishnu that whoever
finds the head or foot of his form of flame would be considered
greatest. Then Brahma took the form of a swan and set out to
reach the top of the flame. Vishnu took the form of a boar to
seek out the foot of the fire. But, in spite of their efforts, they
could not succeed in finding the limits and they both
surrendered to Shiva. This shows how Shiva cannot be
approached through ego but responds with love to those who
surrender to him. To exhibit Shiva's greatness, devotees started
worshiping that cosmic pillar of fire as Linga, i.e. a column. This
also corroborates the meaning of Lingam in Sanskrit as 'evidence
or proof'. This form of Shiva is called Lingodbhava.

Physically a Linga (commonly known as Shivaling) is a phallic
symbol, representing the male and female sexual organs in a state
of marital bliss. Mentally it symbolizes the union of mind and
body. Spiritually it represents the union between Purusha and
Prakriti, the highest principles of the universe. Universally, it
stands for life and existence, the coming together of matter and
consciousness, of gross bodies and subtle bodies to create the
life.

Another explanation is that Shiva means auspicious. So,
the linga is the shapeless symbol for the great god of
auspiciousness. It is intended to bring the shapeless unknown
into our attention. The lingam is essentially a symbol of the
shapeless universal consciousness of Lord Shiva. It is a

representative of the dormant universal consciousness in which all created things rest after the cosmic annihilation.

In Shaivism, lingam means complete Brahman. In most temples, the lingas are formed in three parts. The lowest part is the base square called the Brahma-bhaga, which represents the creator Brahma. The next part in the middle is the octagonal Vishnu-bhaga which signifies Lord Vishnu the preserver. Both these parts form the pedestal. The top cylindrical portion is the Rudra-bhaga or Shiva-bhaga, which is also called the Puja-bhaga since this is the part for worshipping. The top portion is also meant to symbolize the projecting flame of fire. This flame also represents the destructive aspects as well as the preserving power of God.

6.2   Need of destroyer and dissolution

In line with previous two chapters, and considering Shiva as Lord of Dissolution, here also we need to consider the three basic questions, i.e.

1- 'Who' is responsible for destruction / dissolution?
2- 'Why' destruction / dissolution of universe needed?
3- 'How' destruction / dissolution is done?

Answer to the question 'Who' is very clear and that is the Brahman, in the form of Lord Shiva. Shiva is not only destroyer of evildoers, but he also destroys ego and all that is evil and negative in the world. And, as the destroyer, it is he who opens a space for the creation of new positive actions, ideas and pathways. Shiva, as benefactor, also destroys ego, ignorance and other impurities in mind of individuals thru his role as teacher (Dakshinamurthy) and yogi and thru such destruction, Shiva paves way for individuals for spiritual evolution and finding balance within one's self and learning the difficult art of detachment. He transforms the demonic nature hidden in creation to facilitate order and regularity and the liberation of living beings.

The question 'why dissolution / destruction' has partly been answered above. He destroys all the worlds at the end of creation and dissolve them into nothingness to pave way for a new creation by Brahma. Chapter-2 has already mentioned of a 'Big Crunch' when all the energy of universe will be finished and the universe will shrink into nothingness, thus paving way for next 'Big Bang'. Shiva does the same thing. Even before the arrival of 'Big Crunch', i.e. end of universe, Shiva continues his task of destruction / dissolution of many things in order to ensure the order of the universe. His destruction is not negative. It is a positive, nourishing and constructive destruction which builds and transforms life and energy for the welfare of the world and the living beings that inhabit it. He destroys in order to renew and regenerate life forms and facilitate the transformation, evolution or modifications of Nature. He destroys our attachments, impurities, physical and mental wrong doings, the effects of bad karma, our passions and emotions and many things which stand between us and God as hindrance to our progress and inner transmutation.

Shiva has a darker side too. He has been the object of worship by many schools of tantra, some of whom follow sexual cults and other the negative paths in search of self-realization. Many occult practitioners also show Shiva (sometime goddess Kali) as their source. The fact is that with his unlimited wisdom and boundless love as a World Teacher and Father of all, Lord Shiva, gives immense freedom to his followers to choose whatever path they want to follow for their self-realization.

The 3rd question 'How; would be discussed in subsequent paragraphs.

6.3   Organization Chart & functioning of Lord Shiva

Five forms of Shiva (Panchanana), as per Shaivism, has been mentioned in Sec.6.1. The Vedas and few Puranas speak of the 'Ashta Murthys' (8-forms) of Lord Shiva, which are Sharva (Bhoomi Linga), Bhava (Jala Linga), Rudra (Agni Linga), Ugra (Vayu Linga), Bheema (Akaasha Linga), Pasupathi

(Yajamana Linga), Mahadeva (Chandra Linga,) and Eashana (Surya Linga), located at different places in India and Nepal. The essential qualities / attributes associated with all the eight murthys / forms are destroyer of darkness and evil, creation, dispeller of sorrows, the fearsome, the tremendous, Lord of all beings, the supreme and the directional ruler, respectively. These 8 forms of Shiva also stand for five elements plus the soul, the sun and the moon. Few other scriptures give yet many other forms of Shiva.

Occasionally Shiva reveals himself partly or significantly, to perform specific functions for the order and regularity of creation, welfare or dissolution of the worlds. We consider such appearances as his emanations or partial manifestations. Shiva does not have specific and accepted avatars like Lord Vishnu, but these emanations / manifestations, either in full or part (ansh) may be treated as avatars. Few of these emanations/avatars are Hanuman, Nandi, Veerbhadra, Bhairava, Ashwatthama, Grihapati, Durvasa, Rishabh, Pippalada, Yatinath, Bhikshuvarya, Sureshwar, Vaishyanath, Keerat, Suntantarka, Brahmachari, Yaksheshwar, Avadhuteshwar, Sharabh and Dakshinamurthy etc. The difference between the forms of Lord Vishnu and Shiva is that in case of Lord Vishnu, Avatar means coming down, (Lord Vishnu is, mostly, born and the lineage is found), whereas, in the case of Shiva, it is not clearly found. Many of Shiva's emanation appears, does what he has to do and disappears.

All these show the magnanimity and greatness of Lord Shiva. However, for our limited purpose of this book, we have grouped all the forms and emanations of Shiva in five categories, as shown in figure F-6.1 (Simplified organization chart of Lord Shiva for destruction), covering all the destruction / dissolution jobs of Lord Shiva.

1- Anugrahamurthy & Saumya-murthy- Milder, happy and peaceful aspect of Lord Shiva when he is in the company of his beloved devotees or his family members.

2- Dakshinamurthy- A universal teacher, teaching the
secrets of yoga, tantras, yantras, alchemy, magic, occult
knowledge, arts and sciences, ancient history or
knowledge of the future to the sages and saints, gods and
goddesses and his highly qualified devotees. He is called
Dakshinamurthy, because he does his teachings sitting
on the snowy mountains of Himalayas and facing
towards the Indian subcontinent, which is in the
southerly direction.

3- Ugramurthy (Samharamurthy)- It is the ferocious or
angry form of Shiva, associated with his destructive form
to slay the demons and wicked of the world. Many of
these forms, Shiva had to take, because the demons he
had to kill, had taken boon from Shiva himself and, as
such, he could not kill them in his normal form. These
includes:

a- Kankala-bhairava- The form he assumed when he
cut off the fifth head of Brahma.

b- Gajasura-vadha-murthy- The form he assumed while
killing a demon, named Nila.

c- Tripurantakmurthi- The form he assumed when he
destroyed the cities of gold, silver, and iron built by
three sons of Andhakasura.

d- Sarabhesa-murthy- The form in which he allegedly
fought, killed and liberated Narasimha, the
incarnation of Vishnu, after Narasimha had done his
job.

e- Kalari-murthy- The form Shiva assumed to fight and
defeat Yama to save his devotee Markandeya.

f- Kamantaka-murthy- The form in which Shiva
destroyed Manmadha (Kamadeva), the god of lust,
for disturbing him while doing penance.

g- Andhakasura-vadha-murthy- The form in which
Shiva defeated Andhakasura, who, later, joined his

forces as his commander and became popular as
Bhringi.

h- Bhairava-murthy (Mahakal Bhairava)- The form of
Shiva associated with annihilation and generally
found in connection with the secret cults of Tantrism
that involve his worship in the cremation grounds
and grave-yards.

i-   In addition to Shiva himself taking ugra-murthy
form to destroy evil doers, his consort,
Shakti/Parvati, takes different Ugra / ferocious
forms (like Kali, Durga, Chandi etc.) to destroy few
evil doers, thus actively helping or participating with
Shiva in destruction.

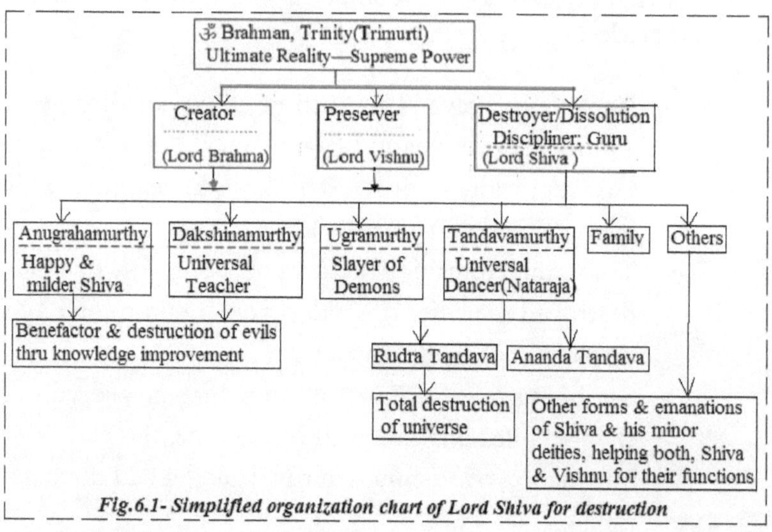

Fig.6.1- Simplified organization chart of Lord Shiva for destruction

4- Tandavamurthy (Nritya-Murthy)- It is the dancing form
of Shiva. About nine forms of Shiva in dancing mode are
described, of which the most popular form is Nataraja
(the king of dance). Through his dance, he sets in motion
numerous vibrations which are vital to the continuation
of the worlds. Shiva's dance is his act of creation or
destruction in a dynamic rhythmic movement. Two main
forms are Anand-Tandava (in a pleasant and cheerful

mood) and Rudra-Tandava (when destroying the whole universe). Shiva does Rudra Tandava when he is very angry, either because of some unpleasant situation like when his consort Sati jumped into 'Agni-kund' (sacrificial fire) because of her father Daksha not respecting Shiva, or incident like killing dwarf demon Apasmara (said to be a symbol of ignorance and arrogance) or whenever the universe is to be dissolved at the end of cycle (Brahma-day). Rudra-Tandava is, sometimes, called 'kaali-Tandava". In all, Shiva's Tandav (Nataraja) dance has 5 principles- 'Srishti' (creation, evolution), 'Sthithi'(preservation), 'Samhara' (destruction/ dissolution), 'Tirobhava' (illusion) and 'Anugraha' (release, grace).

Puranas give some details how Shiva assists in the cosmic annihilation, while doing Rudra-Tandava, towards the end of Brahma-day. A great scarcity of food occurs. Lord Vishnu also assumes the form of Shiva and enters in the sunrays, making it so hot that the whole world (the three planetary systems) dries up. As Vishnu has entered in Shiva, the scorching breath of Ananta Sesha also reduces the lower planetary system of Pataala to ashes. A vast whirlpool of flame then spreads to the higher region of the demigods and puts them all to ruin. Few others say that Lord Shiva's Tandava dancing causes such a commotion that it brings in the clouds that cause the universe to become inundated with water and the whole world is submerged in that deluge.

5- Others- It includes few other forms / murthys / emanations of Shiva such as Lingodhbhava-murthy, Bhikshatana-murthi, Ardhanariswara, Hridaya-murthy, and few minor deities such as Nandi, Bhringi, Chandesvara, etc. Various emanations (sometimes called avatars) mentioned earlier in this section also come in this category. The 12 Jyoti-lings and the Pashupatinath of Nepal can also be said as emanations of Shiva. Of-course some of these are not directly associated with Shiva's role as destroyer.

We can bring-out some similarity between Vishnu's and Shiva's way of working. Anugrahamurthy, Saumya-murthy and Dakshinamurthy may be considered for 'general dissolution', Ugramurthys for 'advanced dissolution' and Rudra Tandav for 'intensive dissolution'. His family and others also fit in both general dissolution and advanced dissolution.

6.3.1   Family of Lord Shiva

Shiva's family is unique and somewhat mysterious. Shiva's family is essential part of his organization, as they actively participate in preservation and destruction jobs. Apparently, Shiva appears to have two wives—first one Sati and second one as Parvati. But, actually, Parvati is reincarnation of Sati. When her father Daksha didn't respect her husband Shiva, Sati jumped in fire and took rebirth as Parvati and married again to Shiva. Also known as Shakti, Shiva's wife herself is considered as all-powerful Aadi-Shakti or Mother Goddess. She has taken about ten forms for different functions, few of which (Durga, Kali, Chadrika or Devi Chandi etc.) killed different demons and, thus, helped Shiva in destruction / dissolution job.

Most people believe that Shiva has two sons (Kartikeya and Ganesh) and one daughter (Ashok Sundari). Kartikeya (also known as Murugan, Skanda, Kumara and Subrahmanya) was born from Shiva's semen and raised by six mothers for special purpose for killing demon Tarkasur. Ganesh was created by Parvati as a normal boy, using earth. Due to some misunderstanding, Shiva cut the head of Ganesh, but later installed the head of an elephant instead and made him most intelligent and first worshipped deity.

However, some believe that Shiva has six sons not only two. The 4 other sons, not born directly thru Parvati, are as follows-

1- Ayyapa (also known as Sastav), born after Shiva married
   Mohini, the female avatar of Lord Vishnu. Worshipped
   much in South India.

2- Andhaka (Andhakasura)- Some scriptures say that he was
   born from Shiva's sweat. He was born blind. He, later,
   tried to abduct Parvati and, so, was defeated by Shiva in
   Tripurantakmurthi form.

3- Bhauma- He was also born of Shiva's sweat. As the
   sweat fell on earth, goddess Bhumi (Earth) nurtured him,
   hence named Bhauma. He, later, became deity Mangal.

4- Khuja- He was born when the powerful ray of energy
   was emitted from Shiva's chest during meditation. It is
   also said that Bhauma and Khuja were the same and
   deity Mangal (planet Mars) stands for both.

5- Shiva also had another daughter, Mansa, who was born
   when Shiva's semen touched the statue of snake's
   mother. Mansa is a deity who cures snake bites.

6.4   Shiva's way vs Corporate I/c General Administration

Just like Vishnu does his preservation in three ways, general
care, advanced care and intensive care, Shiva also does his
destruction / dissolution job in three ways—

1- Destruction of evils (ego, ignorance and other impurities
   in mind of individuals) by knowledge improvement thru
   his Anugrahamurthy and Dakshinamurthy forms (general
   dissolution).
2- Minor destruction of evils & evil doers by taking various
   Ugramurthy forms, depending upon case of evil doers
   (advanced dissolution).
3- Major or total destruction of universe towards the end of
   Brahma Day, i.e. end of the cycle of universe, or
   otherwise as needed, by taking the Rudra-Tandava form
   of Tandavamurthy (intensive dissolution).

4- The 4th category may be special, such as drinking Halahal (poison) and storing in his throat to save the whole world and, also, helping indirectly preservation of universe.

Shiva's this way of working can be considered as similar to Corporate I/c, General Administration. This has been shown in Table T-6.2, which is self-explanatory.

Table T-6.2- Shiva's way of working vis-a-vis Corporate I/c General Administration

Functions \ Doers	Shiva, the destroyer for dissolution of universe	Corporate I/c, General Administration
Destruction of bad practices & evils thru knowledge improvement	Thru Anugrahamurthy & Dakshinamurthy, Shiva destroys the ego, ignorance and other impurities in mind of individuals	Employees knowledge & skill Development, Physical fitness, yoga & mindfulness etc.to remove bad practices and pave way for better.
Minor destruction of evils & evil doers	Destroying the evils and evil doers by taking different ugramurthy forms.	Security, discipline, judging, punishment; also, minor restructuring & down-sizing or merger of units / facilities.
Total destruction of universe	Destroying whole or major portion of universe.	Total decommissioning, breakage and disposal or relocation of existing unit & land rehabilitation to prior state for any new unit.
Others, as per need	Drinking Halahal (poison) & storing that in throat to save the world; Helping	Helping I/c Works & Plant as per need thru existing facilities

	Vishnu in preservation job thru Ganesha, Hanuman etc.	

6.4.1   Shiva's approach to bad corporate practices

Bad practices are covert killers. Since their effects are subtle and slow, one may not realize that a practice, implemented years ago, is making company's innovation pipeline run dry and the employees getting demotivated or unprepared or frustrated. Lord Shiva's principle of destroying or eliminating bad practices can be applied in any corporate entity in the sequence or manner mentioned above. Bad practices, such as absenteeism, poor turnover, low job satisfaction, lack of involvement and obsolete or suspicious or risky practices that may weaken the organization, need to be weeded out. Workflows to be studied, and bureaucratic obstacles or paperwork blocks are eliminated or reduced. Only by eliminating bad practices, new values and practices can be put into place and be nurtured. Knowledge/ skill improvement is the first step to remove bad practices. Serious actions like disciplinary action and minor restructuring can be taken as per need. Catastrophic action, like total closure etc. may be essential only when all other measures don't yield desired result.

6.5   Shiva's management of contradicting attributes

Shiva appears to be a god of ambiguity and paradox; whose attributes include opposing themes. As shown in Sec. 6.1, Shiva, as destroyer, has predominantly "Tamasic Guna", but as Ishana, his "Sattvic Guna" is dominant. Thus, Shiva manifests himself in two opposite forms which contradict each other. Few such contradicting examples are given below, which will help us in understanding and taking right action in our daily life as, often, we also are placed in contradicting situations. Also, all these are very important for the executives / employees in any corporate entity.

1- Fierceness and Auspiciousness- One name of Shiva is
   'Rudra' which means 'fierce' or 'terror'. Another name of
   Shiva is 'Ishana' which means 'auspicious', 'bliss'. Now
   how can auspicious and terror exist together? Well, a
   corporate employee has to develop that.

2- 'Destruction and affection' or 'Destroyer and
   Benefactor'- On one hand, he is destroyer and on other
   hand, he is also 'Pasupati' or Lord of creatures and
   Sankara (Giver of Pleasure). Now how can a destroyer
   become their Lord and give pleasure? We have to learn
   and practice that in our life and work.

3- Attachment and Detachment- He is detached from
   everything. He is the ideal for sanyasis. But he cries when
   Sati self-immolated. How can a detached person cry and
   become like a mad / angry person? A corporate
   employee should be attached to company's principles,
   ethics and goal, but should be detached from his
   personal interest in those.

4- Moha / Kama and no-Kama situation- Shiva himself is
   the destroyer of 'Kama" but he falls in love with Mohini?
   How can a destroyer of Kama be attracted towards
   Mohini? This also helps un in managing contradicting
   situation.

5- Sattvic and Tamasic- Shiva smears himself with ash of
   cemetery, lives with Ghosts and Pisachas which are
   tamasic and considered impure. But the purest Ganga is
   flowing from his head. They are existing together.

6- Ascetic and householder - On one hand, Shiva is
   dispassionate yogi / sanyasi / renunciant and on other
   hand he is considered as ideal husband and also a
   passionate lover. Again, family of Shiva is very
   mysterious. Vahana (riding vehicle) of Ganesh is mouse.
   Vahana of Shiva is Ox. Vahana of Kumara is Peacock.

Vahana of Parvati / Durga is considered Cat / Tiger. Now, let us see. Cat eats mouse. Tiger eats Ox. Peacock eats snake and rat. But they live mutually in family of Shiva. A very good lesson for us.

7- Dance- Shiva's dance are of two types- the Anand-Tandava (the gentle form of dance), associated with the creation of the world, and the Rudra-Tandava (the violent and dangerous dance), associated with the destruction of world or weary worldviews. In essence, both are just the two aspects of Shiva's nature.

6.6   Difference between Vishnu and Shiva as destroyer

Vishnu is the preserver, and Shiva the destroyer, but they are both destroyers of evildoers and protectors of the world. The Truth here is, there is no difference between Vishnu and Shiva. Shiva is none other than Vishnu, and Vishnu is none other than Shiva. That is why their actions seem identical, for they are the same. However, considering Vishnu and Shiva as two different identities for destruction job, let us explore what is the difference between the two. The difference related to appearance, abode, habit, personalities and activities etc. between Vishnu and Shiva have been discussed separately. Here we will narrow-down only on the aspects of destruction of evil and evil-doers.

1.   As far as difference in path is concerned, Vishnu path is mainly based on devotion. A strict follower of Vishnu can be seen doing Kirtan & dancing by chanting Hari-nam. Shiva path is mainly based on meditation. A strict follower of Shiva can be seen immersed in 'Samadhi' in lonely places or doing 'Dhyan' by chanting Aum Namah Shivaya. Vishnu signifies the intense 'Bhakti' (devotion) of a devotee towards God throughout his life while Shiva signifies a devotee's will to realize the God by constantly meditating upon him & by being detached from earthly happenings.

2. Vishnu preserves life on earth by destroying evil by love
    (e.g. few minor avatars) or war (e.g. his major avatars).
    He destroys as per need and gives a hint, as Krishna,
    that everything is fair in love and war. As such, though
    Vishnu also destroys, he is still called preserver. Shiva
    destroys the entire existence through his dancing,
    paving a way for recreation. Shiva destroys the old
    order altogether so a new universe or culture can be
    formed. He also destroys few demons, causing serious
    destruction/disturbance in universe in order to take
    care of the damages due to the boon given to the
    demons by Brahma or Shiva himself. We can also say
    that he destroys limited perceptions and habits so one
    can achieve spiritual renewal and achieve higher
    dimensions. Shiva's opening of his third eye can not
    only be seen as destroying the world but opening to
    greater heights which make the old seem worthless and
    to be done away with.

3. Vishnu is said to support mainly the Devas, while Shiva
    is said to support both Devas and Asuras (Demons).
    When the demons, after getting boons from Shiva,
    disturbs the dharma and life on Earth or elsewhere, it
    can only be Vishnu to destroy them. How can Shiva kill
    his own Bhakt? That would directly contradict Shiva's
    role as a God. The arrangement between Vishnu and
    Shiva is such that all demons get boons easily from
    Shiva (or also from Brahma) and get killed by Vishnu
    after they do their function of creating necessary
    tension and stress for people.

4. Asuras want invincible powers to defeat Vishnu,
    mostly. By giving boons to Asuras, Shiva has set the
    destruction in motion. Similarly, Brahma does it too.
    Once a devotee (including demons), undergoes the
    rigors of Tapasya / penance and completes that
    satisfactorily, giving boons to them (esp. demons) by
    Brahma or Shiva is compulsion for them, even knowing
    that the demons may misuse the boon for disturbing

peace. If the Lords refuse giving the demons boon of extraordinary power etc., the very virtue and sanctity of Tapasya / penance will decrease, if not lost and people in general will feel discouraged to take Tapasya route.

5. Vishnu, being the Preserver, has the Dharma of destroying evil to establish Dharma. Both, Shiva and Brahma, uses Maya (illusion) to make Asuras think that he is their support, while he actually has set in motion their destruction. Vishnu uses his Maya to fool and confuse the Asuras (like he did as Mohini), before destroying them.

6. As per one legend, once when human's wickedness overran all limits, Shiva got infuriated and transformed himself into a wrathful form known as Bhairava. Thus converted, Shiva began his rampage of destruction, killing and ripping out hearts of humans and drinking blood, his menacing laughter thundering all-around. After being pacified by Vishnu, Shiva told Vishnu "So long as you preserve the world, I will not seek to quench my thirst. But when the world becomes so corrupt that even you cannot sustain it, I will raise my trident and squeeze every drop of blood from the heart of human".

As, often, Shiva and Vishnu work and help each other in their jobs, the name Harihara is the fused representation of Vishnu (Hari) and Shiva (Hara). Similarly, Shankaranarayana stands for "Shankara" as Shiva, and "Narayana" as Vishnu. As such these are worshipped by both, Vaishnavites and Shaivites as a form of the Supreme God.

6.7   Iconography of Lord Shiva

Presenting iconography of Shiva is rather difficult, as he is portrayed and worshiped in many differing forms, a few of which are given herewith---

a- One who is almost naked ascetic who has even
    conquered over Kama,

b- One who he's worshiped as a passionate lover and is
    worshiped along with his consort Shakti as the union,

c- One in a pacific mood with his consort Parvati and son
    Skanda and Ganesh,

d- One as the cosmic dancer (Nataraja),

e- One as a mendicant beggar or as a yogi,

f- One as the androgynous union of Siva and his consort in
    one body, half-male and half-female (Ardhnarishwar),

g- Linga form; this has become more popular, probably,
    because of vagueness and variations in other forms.

The essential prerequisites for Shiva, as destroyer, are
knowledge and power. Shiva has abundance of both as his own
plus he has the support and power of Shakti / Parvati, who
herself is all powerful. Again, Shiva is mostly portrayed in sitting
(Padmasana / Lotus) position, though sometimes in standing or
dancing postures. Sometimes he is depicted very benevolent and
sometime very fearsome. Many fearsome forms are given in
Sec.6.3. Another of Shiva's fearsome forms is as 'Kala' (time)
and 'Mahakala' (great time), which ultimately destroys all things.
Considering broadly the forms (a) to (f) above, the attributes of
Shiva can be as followings---

1- His abode is, normally, Mount Kailash (earlier Mount
    Meru), though he is present everywhere. In Hindu
    mythology, Mount Kailash is conceived as resembling
    a Linga, representing the center of the universe.
    Sometimes Shiva is shown sitting in cremation ground. It
    signifies that he is the controller of death in physical
    world.

    Sometime a question is raised that, if Brahma's abode is
    Brahma-Lok (Satya-Lok) and Vishnu's abode is given as
    'Vaikuntha-Lok, both heavenly abodes, why Shiva's
    abode is given on Mount Kailash on Earth (Bhu-Loka)?

One reason for that is given that, while devas/demigods and demons can easily reach Bramha-Lok and Vaikuntha-Lok, because of their special power, Humankind of Earth can't go to the abode of Brahma and Vishnu. So, Lord Shiva chose his abode on Earth (Mount Kailash), so that even Humans can visit Shiva. This again shows the magnanimity of Lord Shiva.

2- Third Eye- Shiva is often depicted with a third eye (between two eyebrows) with which he burned Kama (Desire) to ashes. It is the eye of wisdom, by opening which he destroys not only fierce demons but also our false selves and our myriad illusions.

3- Crescent Moon- Shiva bears on his head the crescent of the moon. The placement of the moon on his head as a standard iconographic feature dates to the period when Rudra rose to prominence and became the major deity Rudra-Shiva. Legends also say that when moon came out from sea during samundra manthan (churning of ocean), Shiva adorned that moon on his head.

4- Jata (Matted Hair): The flow of his matted hair, which is somewhat shaggy or curly, represents Shiva as the Lord of Wind or Vayu, who is the subtle form of breath present in all living beings.

5- Sacred Ganga- The holiest of the holy rivers, Ganga flows from the matted hair of Shiva. Shiva absorbed the force of Ganga, falling from heaven, and allowed an outlet to that to traverse the earth and bring purifying water to human being. Ganga also denotes fertility - one of the creative aspects of the Rudra/Shiva.

6- Ashes & Vibhuti- Shiva's unclad body, covered with ashes (bhasma), symbolizes the transcendental aspect of Shiva. The ashes represent a reminder that all of material existence is impermanent, comes to an end and becomes ash. Vibhuti is a three line of ashes drawn on the forehead that signifies the immortality of the soul and manifested glory of the Lord.

7- Half-Open Eyes- The half-open eyes show that the cycle of universes is in process. When the eyes are completely closed it signifies the dissolvent of the universe and when it is completely open, a new cycle of creation begins.

8- Blue Throat (Neelkantha)- Shiva's blue throat shows that he drank and stored in his neck, the halahal (poison / toxin) to save the world by eliminating the destructive capacity of poison.

9- Kundalas (2 Earrings)- Shiva is, often, shown, as wearing two kundalas in his years, alakshya (i.e. which can't be shown by any sign) and 'niranjan (i.e. which can't be seen by mortal eyes) and that signifies that he is beyond ordinary perception. The kundela in Shiva's left ear is of the type normally worn by women and that in his right ear is of the type, generally worn by men. Thus, the kundalas symbolize the Shiva and Shakti, i.e. masculine energy and feminine energy concept for creation.

10- Cobra Necklace- This suggests that Shiva is beyond the powers of death and is often the sole support in case of distress. The cobras around his neck also represent the dormant energy, called Kundalini, the serpent power. The snake curled three times around the neck of Lord Shiva depicts the past, present and future time.

11- Rudraksha Necklace- 'Rudra' means uncompromising and 'aksha' means 'eye'. Rudraksha necklace worn by Shiva means that he uses the cosmic laws firmly, without compromising, to maintain the law and order of universe. The 108 beads necklace symbolizes the elements used in the creation of world. In few depictions, rudraksha necklace is shown as rosary beads in Shiva's right hand.

12- Trident (Trisula)- The three-pronged trident, shown adjacent to Shiva, symbolizes his three fundamental powers (shakti), i.e. 'Ichha' (will or desire), 'Kriya' (action) and 'Gyana' (knowledge). It also represents the three gunas (Sattvic, Rajas and Tapas). As a weapon, the trident represents the instrument of punishment to the evildoer on all the three planes - spiritual, subtle and physical.

13- Tiger Skin- Shiva is shown sitting on or wearing a tiger skin. The tiger is the vehicle of Shakti, the Goddess of power and force. Shiva is beyond and above any kind of force. The tiger skin that he wears symbolizes victory over every force. Tiger also represent lust. Thus, sitting on tiger skin, Shiva indicates that he has conquered lust. Few depictions also show elephant skin.

14- Damaru (Drum)- It is a small drum shaped like an hourglass, with two sides alienated from each other by a thin neck-like structure. It represents the two utterly different states of existence, unclear(unmanifest) and clear (manifest). When a damaru is shaken, it produces two dissimilar sound, which are fused together by resonance producing a sound called 'Nada', the cosmic sound of AUM, which can be heard during deep meditation also.

15- Kamandalu- A water pot (Kamandalu), made from dry pumpkin, containing nectar, is shown on the ground next to Shiva. Yogis and saints use kamandalu to store clean water for drinking. The process of making Kamandalu from pumpkin signifies an individual whose inside has been cleaned of egoistic desires.

16- Nandi (the Bull)- Nandi is associated with Shiva and is also his vehicle. The bull signifies both power and ignorance. Shiva using the bull as his vehicle conveys the idea that he removes ignorance and bequeaths power of wisdom on his followers. Nandi (also called Nandiswara) is humility personified.

Like Vishnu, Shiva is also known by over thousand names (Shiva Sahasranama). Few of those have already been mentioned earlier. Few other notable ones are Bholenath (kind-hearted Lord), Bhairav (destroyer of fear), Bhutanatha (Lord of Ghosts), Gangadhara (Lord of River Ganga), Pasupathi, (Lord of the animals), Trilochana (Three-eyed), Pancha-anana (Five-faced), Chandrashekhara (Moon-crested), Girisha (Mountain Lord), Mahadeva (Great God), Mritunjaya (conqueror of death), Maheshwara (Lord of Gods), Vishveshwara (Lord of the Universe) and Vishwanath (Master of the Universe) etc.

6.8   Important lessons from Lord Shiva

That Shiva is ultimate Guru or guide can be corroborated from the incidences from Rama Avatar or Krishna Avatars that whenever Rama or Krishna faced some difficult task, they prayed Lord Shiva for help and guidance. Few Basic teachings from Shiva are as follows---

1- Knowledge is God. One person cannot possess the knowledge of everything, but everyone can possess the knowledge of something. We should find that seed of knowledge within us, and then do all our karma around it.

2- Everything is illusion (Maya). What life we are living, at what place we are; if our happiness depends on the materialistic things we own, then happiness is an illusion for us, and it will be gone with that thing. Shiva teaches us not to attach our happiness to earthly things. Learning the art of detachment, while remaining a part of society, works wonders in our family life as well as for any employee in any corporate entity.

3- Look beyond happiness. We must control our ego and let go of our pride. The world, we are living in, is growing more egoistic and individualistic. Everyone is worried about their happiness and doesn't care if people around them are happy or not. However, the real happiness is beyond limits, and it could be felt only when we have found the seed of knowledge within us, and we are truthful with others and ourselves. Happiness comes from within, not outside. Materialistic happiness never stays for long.

4- Be formless. For happy parson, illusion does not control them. Put them in any situation at any place; they will be the same calm and content in their mind. Shiva does the same and teaches us to practice being formless like water.

5- Use all our senses. When our mind is at peace with heart, and we walk towards self-realization, all our senses come together to work in proper synchronization. When we achieve this state in our physical form, the feeling we get is unmatched.

6- Exercise Self-control and keep calm. An uncontrolled personality can lead us to carry on with a distressing life.

7- Respect your better half. Shiva's 'Ardhanarishwar' form induces us to treat our better half with the utmost regard and care and gives the true meaning of matrimony. He also teaches to live, as family, even with people of different nature, like he lives with Ganesh, rat, peacock, snake, bull, cat / tiger etc. (refer Sec.6.5)

8- Concealment of mischief and outrage- Shiva's blue throat, because of drinking poison /toxin in order to save the world, teaches us concealment of mischief and outrage and, if necessary, express in proper way to save the situation.

9- Desires lead to obsessions and obsessions lead to destruction. Since Shiva is free from desires, he is never obsessed over things. Desires always lead to obsessions, and these in turn make us self-destructive.

10- Enlightenment is awakening. If we do good karma, we can attain the enlightenment, the highest form of existence for a human. In this state of mind, we achieve self-realization along with the proper understanding of nature and reality.

6.9   The three faces of Brahman and impact on our life

The table T-6.3, roughly gives the broad comparison of the three faces of Brahman, i.e. Brahma, Vishnu and Shiva, derived mainly from the previous discussions in this book.

Table T-6.3 - Broad comparison of three faces/forms of Brahman

#	Lord Brahma (I/c Planning & Creation)	Lord Vishnu (I/c Preservation & Maintenance)	Lord Shiva (I/c Discipline & Dissolution)
1	Most Knowledgeable (has Goddess Sarasvati/ Vidya as his consort)	Most Resourceful (has Goddess Lakshmi as his consort)	Most Powerful (has Goddess Shakti/ Parvati as his consort)
2	I/c of science & engineering	I/c of commerce, politics & overall management	I/c of arts, yoga, discipline & dissolution
3	Lord of positiveness & kindness (even Lord Vishnu & Lord Shiva worship Lord Brahma for positiveness)	Lord of righteousness & success (even Lord Brahma & Lord Shiva worship Lord Vishnu for success)	Lord of Justice & fitness (even Lord Brahma & Lord Vishnu worship Lord Shiva for fitness)
4	He is Jeevan-daata, i.e. creates or gives birth to life.	He is Anna-daata & Sukh-daata, i.e. gives food and happiness	He is discipliner & Mrityu-daata (one who annihilates) & also Yogi and teacher
5	Overlord of Sapta-rishis and all other	Overlord of Incorporeal Avatars /	Overlord of few incorporeal avatars

	rishis and munis / saints.	Deities, e.g. Indra, Surya, Agni, Varun deo, Vayu deo etc.	(Shani Deo & Yama-raj), Nag-raj & all Bhutas & Pishachas.
6	Rajasic Guna	Sattvic Guna	Tamasic Guna as destroyer & Sattvic Guna as benefactor
7	Works by creating sons & daughters; no avatars	Works with many Incorporeal, major and minor avatars. Sons/daughters not much involved.	Shiva doesn't have specific avatars like Vishnu but has many deities or forms as his 'ansh'/emanations. He works directly or indirectly by taking different forms.
8	Gets easily pleased, even by demons.	Doesn't get easily pleased by demons. He does anything to protect dharma and doesn't care who you are. If you're wrong, then you're wrong. (ex: Bali & Banasur)	Gets easily pleased even by demons. He tries to protect his devotees, even after knowing that they are misusing his boons, or they are wrong (ex: Banasur).
9	Consort Sarasvati plays passive & supporting role	Consort Lakshmi plays passive & supporting role	Consort Shakti plays active & participating role & takes different form in different role.

The creation, preservation and dissolution functions of the three Gods are responsible for our existence, continuation, transformation, purification and liberation. Actually, the three qualities of Brahma, Vishnu and Shiva are always present in everyone and works differently at different times. As an example, a police officer on a festival day goes to temple with traditional dress and we can see a totally different pious nature in him (somewhat attribute of Brahma). The same officer while dealing with the issues of administration of family or office will be found with lot of balance and calm mind to solve the problems (somewhat attribute of Vishnu). The same officer while going to attack the terrorists along with his team looks totally in a different way with emotion and valor (somewhat attribute of Shiva). Similar situation may occur in all walks of life, including the person working in any corporate entity. The difference in the situations and functions change the atmosphere even though the same person is involved. Realization of the same one unimaginable God (Brahman) in all the divine personalities with imaginable medium to the imaginable world in both energy and human is the climax of spiritual knowledge.

~~~~~~~~~~~~~~~~~~~~~~
~~~~~~~~~~~~~~~~~~~~~~

Bibliography & References

1- 'The Origin of Universe', lecture by Stephen W. Hawking in 1988 and later

2- 'Grand Design' by Stephen Hawking & Leonard Mlodinow, published by Bantam Books, New York in 2010

3- 'How the universes created & our purpose in it'- by Stephen Knapp, published by Stephen Knapp, The World Relief Network (December 2000)

4- 'Why Be a Hindu: The Advantages of the Vedic Path', posted by Stephen Knapp in August 2009

5- 'Natural Corporate Management: From the Big Bang to Wall Street', By William C. Frederic, Greenleaf Publishing Ltd, Sheffield, UK, in 2012

6- 'Environmental Management in Organizations'- The IEMA Handbook, By John Brady; By Institute of Environmental Management & Assessment (IEMA), Published by Earthscan, UK, 2005

7- 'Corporate Management, Governance, and Ethics Best Practices', By S. Rao Vallabhaneni, published by John Wiley & Sons Inc, NJ, USA, in 2008

8- 'Yoga, Enlightenment & Perfection'-----Shri Vidyateertha Foundation, Chennai, 2015

9- 'The mysterious universe'-- by James Jeans, published by Cambridge University Press, 1930

10- 'The nature of the physical world'—by Arthur Eddington, published at the University Press, Cambridge, UK, 1948

11- 'Supreme God: Body, Will, Wisdom, and Work'---By Prof. Jitendra Dhoj Khand, published by RoseDog Books, PA, USA in 2011

12- 'Why does the God exist?'- By Jim Holt, published by Liveright Publishing Corporation, NY, in 2013

13- The Upanishads Demystified: Ethical values, By Ved Prakash Bhatia, Notion Press, Chennai, 2017

14- Explore Hinduism, by Banshi Pandit, published by Explore Books of Heart of Abion Press, UK, in 2005

15- Sapiens, a Brief History of Humankind' by Yuval Noah Harari, published by HarperCollins Publishers, NY, USA in 2015

16- "You are the Universe' by Deepak Chopra & Means Kafatos; published by Harmony Books, New York, in 2017

17- 'Healing by Reprogramming of Instinctive Mind' by Sushil Kumar Srivastava & Mangla Prasad Srivastava, published by Peacock Books of Atlantic Publishers & Distributors, New Delhi in 2017

18- Website---- http://www.krishna.com/universe-vedas

19- Many other websites and postings on Internet.